THE GOD ADDICTION

AUBREY M. HORTON

Copyright © 2007 by Aubrey M. Horton

All rights reserved, including the right to reproduce this book, or portions thereof, in any form.
Printed in the U.S.A.

Book design and cover photo by Aubrey M. Horton

LIBRARY OF CONGRESS
CATALOGUING-IN-PUBLICATION DATA
on file

ISBN -10:   1448609623
ISBN -13/EAN -13:   9781448609628

First Edition -- 2009

To purchase this book on the Web, go to ->

www.createspace.com/3387597

ScriptDoctor911.com
P.O. Box 2781
Bellingham, WA 98227

to all of those who've suffered from intolerance and hate

CONTENTS

I   Religions Evolved from Shamanistic Thought Addictions   7

II   The Changing Variations of God's Holy Intent   18

III   The Fairy Tale Magic of Religious Dogma   26

IV   Why Has God Made So Many Mistakes?   50

V   The Evolution of Addictive Theology   58

VI   Where Did God Actually Come From?   81

VII   Why Would An Omniscient God Need Anyone to Pray to Him?   90

VIII   Did God Create the Devil, or Did the Devil Create God?   101

IX   The Harmful Benefits of Religious Addiction   114

X   What God Forgot to Tell His Holy Prophets   129

XI   Acclimating to Hidden Knowledge Via Religious Withdrawal   161

I

Religions Evolved from Shamanistic Thought Addictions

To understand why so many people continue to be deceived by flawed beliefs, let us pose the question:

Are there any "general" falsehoods that the public considers to be absolutely true without any doubt whatsoever . . .

But which are, in fact, untrue?

In other words, what controlling superstitions do most people smugly assume to be absolutely true in this moment in time . . .

That will eventually be proven to be totally false?

Now, some might say, in this day and age of unflappable science . . .

That there would be, within our advanced societies, only a few nonessential manifestations where adults are overly relying on magical thinking, and that most of these inconsequential superstitions would be confined to the uneducated and illiterate.

But is this actually true? For isn't it possible that some of our more widely-accepted modern beliefs are, in fact, inaccurate . . .

Simply because it's highly probable that we haven't fully developed the scientific capability to totally understand all of the complexities of the natural world (or of the cosmos) -- even though we may assume that we have?

Indeed, it should be noted that eighty years ago our medical doctors did not believe that frequent X-rays would cause any harm to the human body. And only seventy years ago there were no governmental concerns about cigarettes causing cancer.

Also, almost fifty years ago any person who breathed asbestos fibers wasn't considered to be at risk for pulmonary illness.

So, per the historical record, at any given moment in time, false assumptions have caused well-educated people to make erroneous decisions . . .

In that history has repeatedly demonstrated that what is thought to be true at any given moment in time, can later turn out to be completely false at some point in the future.

Wasn't it only twenty years ago that many doctors advised us to avoid eating butter and to instead consume trans-fat margarine?

But now, only a couple decades later, our medical establishment has completely flip-flopped on trans-fatty acids. Today our top physicians are lobbying for laws, which will completely ban trans fats from our diets.

So, when one ponders what is, in fact, absolutely true . . .

Without any doubt whatsoever . . .

And for those of us who are wise enough to maintain an open-minded skepticism as to what is true and what is false . . .

Such inquisitive thinkers tend to be more accepting of the possibility that new facts will be uncovered in the future . . .

Which will thus change the opinions of the confirmed experts of today. For what was once thought to be . . .

Undisputable science . . .

Can so easily turn out to be wrong.

Therein, in this regard, for those who read books such as this, and for those who attempt to keep an open mind . . .

These seekers of knowledge will

probably not be shocked by the following statement.

Just as many 21st century parents continue to entertain their preadolescents with the magical thinking . . .

Of the Santa myth . . .

So, too, are the masses being fed magical superstitions via the numerous religious thought systems, which have spread across the world. And though there are many people who consider themselves to be . . .

Well educated . . .

It's still possible for such people to have been deceived in regards to certain ideological truths . . .

Just as the pre-Columbian Aztecs were falsely influenced by the teachings of their superstitious clergy . . .

And just as the American public was erroneously taught that trans-fatty acid was a much better cooking ingredient than butter.

In a word, the so-called experts can be wrong and have been proven to be wrong so many times in the past.

"Eat your margarine. It's good for you."

"Avoid the old lady down the street. She's a witch."

"If we sacrifice a newborn baby, the volcano will not destroy our village."

Yes, throughout history . . .

The public has been misled by various forms of false thinking . . .

Because most people are apt to accept what they've been taught by those in positions of authority, i.e., by those who hold sway over the masses.

And it also should be noted that the educators who instruct the masses . . .

Are dependent upon a replicating system of thought . . .

Because such educators -- without challenging what they've been taught -- will, at times, pass along certain falsehoods that have "more in common" with childhood fairy tales than with scientific fact.

Consider the following. Isn't it true that almost all of the knowledge that the average person has acquired . . .

Has come . . .

Not from personal experience or from a clean slate of practical inquiry . . .

But from a transference from other people via the spoken word or via the printed word or via some form of visual media . . .

For is there any other way for most of us to acquire the vast majority of our hard knowledge other than per learning it from others?

Indeed, isn't that how the average person acquires the many truths that they consider to be undeniable facts?

Yet, conversely -- when someone teaches us that something is true . . .

Without a doubt . . .

Are not these well-meaning "instructors" simply echoing what they, too, were taught by their instructors?

For example, take a historical event. If a high school teacher states that such-and-such happened two hundred years ago . . .

Why are her students so absolutely certain that what she is proclaiming to be true . . .

Is, in fact, undeniably true? Was the teacher actually there when the historical event transpired?

No.

Did the teacher actually see with her own eyes . . .

The historical event as it unfolded . . .

Or did the teacher merely acquire the knowledge from other educators . . .

(Educators who were also taught what had transpired . . .)

Or maybe the teacher simply read about the historical event in a textbook?

Hence, isn't it true that our informed sources (in most such cases) . . .

Are simply repeating what they've been taught by those whom they accept to be duly informed . . .

For isn't this the basis for our well-educated society, in that our advanced social structures are based upon conditioned thought patterns vis-à-vis our tiered educational system . . .

Which has defined and established itself per a proven track record of transferring valid truths to generation after generation?

In other words -- from a very young age, aren't we all conditioned to accept the teachings of the previous generation . . .

And aren't many of us rewarded with economic worth when we learn such teachings from our elders, i.e., when we regurgitate back what has been taught to us via having had it validated by an older generation as an accepted fact?

And so, most people do not even question how these dogmatic truths were initially derived . . .

In that most of us are accepting conformists who are simply happy to go about our everyday lives, repeating what we've been taught . . .

And thus reaping the rewards of our educational system . . .

Without a need to challenge why we've

been taught what we've been taught . . .

Or to even question if these truths (that we've been taught) are, in fact, factual.

Why question what obviously works?

And, in this regard, doesn't the social glue of being reasonably compensated for work performed also serve to reinforce our society's core truths . . .

In that revolutions of thought tend to only occur when a cultural system has broken down and isn't working . . .

Or when there occurs excessive hunger and unrelenting poverty . . .

Or when a huge number of innocent civilians are killed via a war?

For when the masses are motivated by the belief in a better future (for themselves and for their children) . . .

When the masses have reasonably good lives without much want (except for the constant pull of unneeded luxuries) . . .

There rarely arises a sustainable need to challenge the conformity of a social system.

Revolutions tend to only occur when a social engine has stopped functioning or when it has lost its efficiency of cooperation. The majority of us (working within a rewarding economy) are not willing to risk a rebellion or risk the life-sustaining necessities that we've garnered via our complacency . . .

Unless there's a perceived fatal social flaw -- which would eventually cause us to lose our lives or livelihoods.

Revolutions tend not to take hold in successful economies where the established thought system is perceived to be working for most of its middle-class citizens.

But it should also be noted that a functioning social system which clearly benefits its members with a rewarding economy . . .

Does not imply that all of the so-called accepted truths of such a society have been proven to be undeniably correct. Historically, many successful societies have had flawed truths embedded within their core beliefs . . .

Yet still these well-performing populations have been able to maintain a fairly high standard of living.

For example, the paganism of ancient Rome relied upon a pantheon of gods and a variety of superstitious rituals (i.e., a web of magical thinking) . . .

Which served as a social glue to control its citizens . . .

And thus -- for hundreds of years the Roman Empire was able to maintain a highly successful ideology . . .

That functioned to motivate its citizenry

and, in the process, allowed for the conquest of large areas of Europe and the Middle East.

Hence, ancient Rome's superstitious dogmas did not hamper its economy. The Roman Empire's high-functioning commercial system was envied the world over. And with few exceptions, Roman citizens lived fairly pleasant lives for a relatively long period of time.

Now, even though most of our present-day scholars would agree that the Romans, before they converted to Christianity, were systemically flawed via their paganism of magical thinking . . .

Few members of the Roman senate (at the time that it existed before Emperor Constantine had his religious conversion to Christianity) would have found fault with their nation's system of pagan beliefs.

Which brings up yet another intriguing question.

How many of our present-day "academics" would've had the willful fortitude to stand up in the Roman senate and challenge the established order . . .

Per declaring that the Roman system of thought . . .

Was based upon false superstitions . . .

And thus such scholars would've been

willing to risk death . . .

If they'd lived in Italy two thousand years ago?

Moreover, to sharpen the focus vis-à-vis personalizing this inquiry . . .

Would you, the reader of this text, have had the courage to challenge such a powerful system of thought, i.e., . . .

Would you yourself have had the will to stand up to the Roman pagans and tell them that their religious system was based upon false superstitions . . .

Knowing full well that you might be killed for your nonconforming rebellion?

II

The Changing Variations of God's Holy Intent

Have you ever wondered why there have been so many variations of God's intent . . .

And why there are so many opposing varieties of religion?

Here's a clue. What personal gain can be achieved by an individual (or a group of individuals) . . .

If they are able to convince others that certain supernatural abilities (and/or beliefs) have been transferred to them by a higher power? In other words, what is in it for the shaman-clerics (i.e., the priests, monks, rabbis, imams, gurus)? Why would these so-called "holy men" want to transfer a superstitious philosophy to the masses if it wasn't true?

Of course, the answer is quite simple. If such clerics can, in fact, fully convince others that they have a unique relationship with God . . .

Then these "religious" practitioners can thus parlay their perceived "supernatural" access into increased personal power, can they not?

For clearly, haven't the priests of the Catholic Church been granted an elevated status over their congregations . . .

Because the Catholic faithful fully believe that their priests are "men of God?" And isn't it also true that many Catholics actually believe that certain members of their clergy have the ability to exorcise demons, to grant special dispensation, and to speak the word of God?

Also, in conjunction with this dogma of faith, haven't the pastors of various Protestant denominations also had similar powers granted unto them?

And don't the members of the Muslim faith also believe that Allah has transferred unique powers to their imams?

And do not the Jewish faithful also believe that God granted their priests and scribes of the first Temple special powers to interpret God's intent?

Now, admittedly -- we pose such rhetorical questions, not to acquire the obvious answers; but, instead, to acquire the hidden knowledge . . .

Which can be derived from the summation of the missing answers . . .

For most would agree that mainstream clerics, when asked certain probing questions, will only answer with the dogma of their "sanitized" doctrines. And these responses will, in many cases, also be highly subjective and thus dependent upon their religious training.

But conversely -- if one seeks a completely objective analysis . . .

Applying scientific logic to such a theological inquiry . . .

Then it is possible to analyze the context of the unanswered questions (and the corollary inconsistencies), which are derived via assessing . . .

The divergent dogmas . . .

Which have been promoted by the various mainstream religions . . .

As one begins to acquire the enlightened knowledge that has, in fact, been hidden from the masses.

Think about this. Isn't it true that most of the world's thought-control systems can be traced back to the implantation of magical thinking . . .

Into our early tribal consciousness via an initiating group . . .

Of shaman-clerics, i.e., . . .

Via the dominating will of a few individuals who were able to usurp such control per the introduction of a "reveled" message . . .

And thus these seminal "holy men" proceeded to claim that they had the unique ability to interact with a higher power?

And didn't the Jewish prophets from the Old Testament believe that God had granted them the supernatural ability to discern future events?

And isn't it also true that Christians believe that Jesus Christ had supernatural abilities granted to him by God; and thus he, the Son of God, was able to turn water into wine, to heal the sick, and to miraculously return from the dead via a crucifixion?

And isn't it also true that Muslims believe that their prophet Muhammad spoke the word of God and was able to, through God's holy intervention, miraculously smite the infidel armies who opposed Muhammad's new religion?

Therein -- when one objectively reviews such examples of religious belief . . .

Which we'll label as magical thinking because there is no verifiable scientific proof that any of the so-called "supernatural" events proclaimed in the Bible or in the Koran actually did, in fact, transpire . . .

And when one also considers the inherent psychology of such magical thinking, in respect to allowing such religious beliefs to gain a foothold within our minds . . .

It becomes clear that there's a repeating scenario, which has continually reoccurred vis-à-vis such religious superstitions in the past . . .

When a small group of elite individuals has been able to consolidate their social power by claiming that they had, in fact, been granted certain "holy abilities" from God (or from a group of gods) . . .

And in consequence to their initiating supernatural claims, when more and more people then proceeded to believe . . .

In these intensely advocated religious declarations . . .

The instigating shaman-clerics (who conceived of these beliefs) were thereupon empowered with an elevated social status and were, many times, also allowed to assume controlling authority over various aspects of a tribe's interactions.

Indeed, isn't this how most, if not all, of the world's religions began? A holy message was claimed to have been initiated by God (or a god) . . .

And then this godly message was said to have been transferred (by a self-proclaimed holy person) to the other members of a tribe.

Of course, if one goes back in time to the prehistoric tipping points when the very first shamans (a.k.a., witch doctors) configured their crude thought systems . . .

So as to be able to explain the random unfolding of natural events . . .

Weren't these early social manipulations relatively easy to integrate into a tribe's consciousness . . .

Due to the fact that primitive tribes were not scientifically educated, and thus they were not able to utilize our present-day forms of critical thinking so as to be able to combat the hypnotic power of magical thinking?

And didn't these early medicine men have much to gain if they could persuade their tribes to believe in their superstitious thought controls? Wouldn't the shaman's social status be duly increased, which would also increase their barter income?

In other words, by assuming the role of the sole communicator with the spirit world, wouldn't a shaman-cleric be able to greatly elevate his tribal power?

Now, unfortunately, as most of us know,

power is addictive and corrupting, is it not? For once a person is able to increase their social power, they also are motivated (by an inner compulsion) to continue to find ways to maintain their power and thus begin to conspire to keep in place the thought mechanisms needed so as to be able to sustain their power over others. One only has to ponder the massive expansions of the world governments throughout the centuries . . .

Or ponder why politicians obsess on more and more lawful control . . .

In order to verify that such a human compulsion truly exists.

So, for the primitive shaman-cleric, there was the personal-gain factor that came into play. By offering magical explanations in response to the unexplained events of nature, a shaman-cleric was able to embed his thought mechanisms into his tribe's consciousness, i.e., . . .

The shaman was able to convince his tribe that he truly had magical abilities.

And thus, when a tribe had been so conditioned to accept a shaman's superstitious applications . . .

Because sometimes it would appear as though a negative event had been reversed via the shaman's magical blessing . . .

(But, of course, this reversal was

nothing more than a natural-cycle probability, in that a normal correction had occurred per a reversal back to a balanced equilibrium from an imbalance state) . . .

The shaman was then able to validate his supernatural power . . .

Claiming that it truly was legitimate.

Now, of course, we're not implying that all of the early shamans had malicious intent or that such "holy men" were totally self-serving per their application of magical cures and thought manipulations. From the historical record, it does appear as though that many, if not most, of the early witch doctors probably had an honest desire to help their tribes (in that helping their tribes also served to help themselves) . . .

And that possibly a majority of these medicine men fully believed in their own magical thinking, however delusional it may've been.

So -- we do believe that these early "priests of nature" were truly motivated to help their tribal congregations.

But having good intentions doesn't validate a supernatural claim . . .

Nor does it prove that a person has a special relationship with God.

III

The Fairy Tale Magic of Religious Dogma

The belief in a supreme being (or beings) can be traced back through the millennia to ancient times. Most of the world's indigenous populations have believed in the existence of one god or of a group of gods . . .

Or they've believed that an overlording spirit (whether personified or not) maintained a supernatural sway over their lives. Also, such god superstitions have been pervasive, in that they have existed in almost all regions of the world.

Consequently, based upon this historical fact . . .

The religious faithful could claim that such a widespread universal compulsion . . .

To believe in a god-force (of whatever

variety) . . .

Serves as proof that God does, in fact, exist. In other words, there must be a God due to the fact that millions of people all over the world have advocated his existence.

But, per this context, is God's existence an undeniably truth; or is his actuality merely a fanciful supposition?

Or, to rephrase the question:

Is man's craving for a parental higher power . . .

Reason enough to accept, without question, the actual existence of an omniscient being?

Note: The human mind has a desire to believe in many things. Simply having a deep longing for an omnipresent god (to make judgments of right and wrong) . . .

Doesn't, in fact, mean that God truly exists . . .

For isn't it also true that many people want to believe that a circus magician can pull a rabbit out of his hat . . .

But most logical-minded people know that such fanciful magic is nothing more than slight of hand? For clearly, the well educated are cognizant of the fact that no human being has the ability to transfer organic (or inorganic) matter from one location to another via a magical force.

Conversely, if someone does believe that a circus performer can "magically" transfer a rabbit into a top hat . . .

Then this belief in the impossible highlights the mesmerizing suggestibility of magical thinking . . .

For there is no way that such a supernatural feat can actually occur or be scientifically proven to occur. Of course there are also numerous people who have a strong desire to believe in voodoo, black magic, and witchcraft. But fortunately, only a small percentage of the world's highly educated are willing to accept even the slightest possibility that such superstitious thought systems are valid. Most of us with college degrees know for a fact that any magical feats associated with the "black arts" are nothing more than fanciful delusions.

Moreover, it should also be noted, in regards to what some might call the quasi-scientific realm of the paranormal . . .

That there are those who believe that UFOs and extraterrestrials do, in fact, exist. And, unfortunately, there are even some highly educated scientists who've gone on record and stated that such sci-fi-ish contemplations have legitimate worth, even though the specifics may be hard to actually prove.

Ergo, taking into consideration such paranormal debates, it can be stated that there is, indeed, a small minority of logical thinkers (within the scientific community) who do actually consider such otherworldly phenomena to have a slim probability of being somewhat possible . . .

And thus such paranormal occurrences can't easily be dismissed as being totally superstitious, although it should be clarified that it's also true that a majority of science-based scholars truly consider such possibilities to be in the same category as that of someone magically pulling a rabbit out of a hat.

So, notwithstanding the slim likelihood that any UFO phenomena will ever be proven to be true, the compulsion by millions of people to believe (without any doubt whatsoever) in such extraterrestrial superstitions seems to substantiate the theory that humans, for some unknown reason, have a predisposition to accept as fact (without scientific proof) that certain forms of supernatural phenomena actually do exist.

Thereupon, some may conclude that mankind has a compulsion to believe in the supernatural . . .

Because this urge to believe in

superstitious thinking seems to be programmed into our DNA, i.e., such paranormal considerations appear to be (for some reason) an inherent configuration of our human nature.

Moreover, many human beings also manifest a natural desire to want to believe in God . . .

And the cause and effect of having such a predisposition hardwired inside our brains is, we think, pivotal to understanding why certain individuals claim to be able to communicate with God (or with the gods) . . .

For we accept the premise that a certain percentage of the religiously obsessed . . .

Do truly believe that they are "chosen" individuals who've been granted a unique ability to understand God's intent . . .

Or to comprehend whatever supernatural force they may choose to refer to the manifestation as being.

And so, it's our opinion . . .

That many such individuals do honestly consider themselves to be spiritually empowered . . .

In that they truly believe that they should be revered by those of us who don't profess to have such godly access.

Of course there's also the nagging possibility that such psychological conditions fall into the mental-illness category and thus tend to occur with individuals who are having delusional thoughts.

Also, it should be pointed out, per this context, that many of the religious believers of today (i.e., the mainstream faithful) seem to have conveniently forgotten that when the earliest religions were first initiated (going back thousands of years) . . .

The world was, at that time, populated by uneducated primitives who could easily be convinced that a supernatural event had legitimately occurred . . .

Simply because a member of their tribe had claimed that they'd seen it happen. For when superstitious falsehoods were first advocated by word of mouth, there were no fact-checking systems or objective investigators or scientific scholars . . .

Or even a logic-based methodology for discerning what was truthful or what was a figment of the imagination . . .

When most of our present-day supernatural beliefs were first introduced.

So if we go back in time to the origins of magical thinking, we must be cognizant of the fact that the primitive humans who first believed in such thought systems . . .

Were woefully undereducated and

highly suggestible . . .

In that, in those ancient times, a tribal member with superior verbal skills and a good imagination . . .

Could convince a fair number of their tribe that a specific superstition was, in fact, absolutely true.

Of course persuading someone that a supernatural event did actually occur required a certain willfulness, but the psychology of such a task wasn't exceptionally demanding before the advent of scientific logic.

Ergo, three thousands years ago, if a shaman-cleric claimed to have been chased by a fire-breathing dragon, then he or she would probably have been believed by their fellow villagers. And, of course, such cases of superstitious tomfoolery were, in fact, fairly common before the evolution of scientific rationalism.

Also, per the historical record, once such a superstitious fiction was generally accepted to be true by the leaders of a tribe . . .

The ego necessity to conform to such a belief would then take hold, and thus the whole tribe would become believers in fire-breathing dragons. Indeed, wasn't this how most magical thoughts achieved legitimacy? A tribal member (such as a shaman-cleric) was able to convince the uneducated members of their tribe that an addictive fantasy was true . . .

And then this socially enforced belief would be transferred from generation to generation (from parent to child). And, consequently, it was via such tribal indoctrinations that the more virulent superstitions eventually evolved into the holy dogmas of the mainstream religions.

Now, per such an assessment, many clerics would dispute this thesis and defend their religious dogmas by claiming that God had to exist due to the overwhelming complexity of life on Earth . . .

For how could there "not" be a God, they would ask? A supreme creator is the only possible explanation for the Earth's well-functioning and highly intricate coordination of life. Our planet's complex web of organic matter is way too complicated . . .

For an all-powerful originator "not" to exist . . .

Is what the religious clerics would have us believe, is it not?

And many rational (and otherwise logical) individuals would also advocate that there has to be a God -- i.e., an intelligent designer -- since this planet's life-force systems . . .

Must have been created by a higher

power due to the trillions of coordinated interactions . . .

Which are required for our ecosystem to properly function and sustain itself.

But wait.

Not so fast.

Could this argument for an intelligent designer be but yet another form of superstitious theology . . .

Or do a majority of the world's top scientists also accept that this intelligent-designer assumption is a verifiable fact?

To further clarify, many people feel (and this includes a certain percentage of our academics) . . .

That a supreme being must have created life on this planet since the existing organisms are way too complex for such an omnificent intelligence not to have been involved in life's creation.

But could there be a more logical explanation?

Here's a clue.

If one believes that the participation of a supreme being is the only way for life to have been created on Earth . . .

Then yet another profound question comes to mind.

If, in order to create intelligent life, there had to have been an intelligent designer (a supreme being, if you will) . . .

Then how was the intelligent designer created, i.e., how did God begin?

In other words, for those who believe that life on Earth could only have been initiated by a god-force . . .

Would these metaphysical speculators also accept the unifying logic of the parallel premise that . . .

If life on Earth could "only" have been created by an intelligent designer . . .

Then this same logic would also imply that the intelligent designer would've had to also have been created by a preceding "supreme" designer in order for the Earth's "intelligent" designer to have come into existence, does it not?

In other words . . .

If life on Earth could only have been created by a supreme being . . .

Then wouldn't the same logic also apply to the initiating creation . . .

Of the supreme being . . .

In that such a mega intelligence would surely have had to have been created by yet another super intelligence, correct?

Now, of course, many of the mainstream dogmatists might respond to such an assessment by stating that God is the exception to such scientific logic. They would argue that

God has "always been and will always be." And most mainstream theologians would also dispute the need for God to have been "created," in that such a thesis is simply, in their minds, a personification of the unknowable . . .

In that most of the faithful believe that human logic can't comprehend God's supernatural existence due to man's limited mental ability.

In other words, religious adherents (per their thought indoctrination) -- have historically been "taught" that they should avoid such theological questions and that it's best to simply rely upon faith when such doubts arise. And, paralleling this advocacy, the mainstream clergy would also have us believe that life on Earth must have been created by an intelligent designer (i.e., by God) . . .

Not because of the obvious fact that a vast number of life forms . . .

Do, in fact, have an overwhelming complexity . . .

But because such hypnotic dogma has been pounded into their heads and has been constantly repeated in the synagogues, churches, and mosques for thousands of years.

Enough said, right?

Wrong.
We disagree.
Not enough said . . .
Because . . .

How can a well-educated modern believer be absolutely positive (without any doubt whatsoever) that such dogmatic suppositions are, in fact, correct . . .

Simply because they've been passed down from generation to generation through the millennia?

Does the frequent repetition of a religious dogma, per thousands of years, generate within such a doctrine a foundation of fact? For example:

For hundreds of years the Roman Catholic Church fully believed and advocated (short of excommunication) . . .

That the Earth was flat and that the Sun revolved around the Earth. And just because millions of people (for hundreds of years) accepted that this holy doctrine was undeniably true, did this truly mean that it was an unquestionable scientific fact?

Indeed, since we've previously established that there's a compelling reason to be highly skeptical of the ego motivations of all shaman-clerics . . .

In that we should always question their religious claims since their social status is dependent upon the naive masses believing in their professed dogmas . . .

Then why should someone be willing to accept the possibility that such an "intelligent-designer" hypothesis is truly correct?

Moreover, when we accept the dogma that "God has always been and will always be" -- doesn't this thought construction clearly eliminate . . .

Any rationalism from the equation . . .

Because by acquiescing to such a system of circular logic, i.e., by blindly assuming that there is a God because many believers can't fathom how life on Earth could've been created without a God . . .

Doesn't the self-serving subjectivity of such an assertion become quite obvious . . .

For isn't such authoritarian dogma, at its crudest form, nothing more than religious propaganda . . .

In that such knee-jerk retorts (to important questions such as this) . . .

Clearly imply that no one has the right to even ask these hard-to-answer theological questions?

And doesn't such a closed authoritarian dogma also reflect upon the clergy's inability to offer a logical response . . .

To such an inquiry . . .

In that it implies that God's faithful administrators feel that they must, instead of offering logical answers to such foundational questions . . .

That they must bully us into completely avoiding such discussions?

Yet, when such questions are asked . . .

The clergy, when cornered to answer, is unable to respond with any scientific proof that can actually substantiate their claim that there exists a spiritual being whose essence doesn't at all conform to the laws of science. For the clergy wants us to believe that there exists a supreme being who, for whatever incomprehensible reason, didn't have a beginning (i.e., didn't have an initiating point and thus is fundamentally contrary to what occurs with all other forms of intelligent existence) . . .

In that the shaman-clerics would have us believe that there exists a God who has the ability to create endless numbers of complex life forms, but who (himself) didn't evolve into his own super-authoritative existence . . .

In that God . . .

They would have us believe . . .

"Always was and always will be" . . .

And thus somehow God came into being without any sort of beginning at all.

Sounds highly suspicious, does it not?

And, amazingly, the masses continue (to this day) to rely upon the goodwill of the shaman-clerics . . .

To help them understand these theological inconsistencies.

So, who's right . . .

And who's wrong?

Here's a clue. What well-credentialed scientist believes (without a doubt) that a highly intelligent creator could spontaneously come into existence?

In other words, is it at all possible for any intelligent life form to instantaneously develop, i.e., to be fully formed and functionally proactive . . .

And also be highly intelligent upon inception?

So, when the intelligent-designer premise is dissected down to its manufactured core . . .

What presents itself is simply an illogical thought speculation.

And yet, the shaman-clerics would have us believe that their Biblical story of God's infinite existence is truthful and undeniable, and that God is a unique supernatural force, i.e., a god-force that doesn't have to conform to the rules of nature . . .

Because, for some unfathomable reason,

no known scientific understanding applies to God's existence . . .

Even though God himself was compelled to create a highly consistent and provable scientific logic . . .

Compelled to generate a rational understanding that humans have been able to apply to all known . . .

Universal mechanisms . . .

But that God, if the faithful believers are correct, specifically chose to exempt himself from such laws of nature.

For, it seems, God is the one exception to the universal application of scientific rationalism . . .

Which he, himself, created.

But does this . . .

"Biblical reasoning" . . .

Seem to be at all logical?

For when we view science's many verifiable systems of interacting molecules . . .

And then when we expand on this understanding . . .

Extrapolating proven logic into the notion that God created an abundance of science-based systems (which few dispute exist) . . .

Yet . . .

When it comes to . . .

God's own existence . . .

His initial creation, if the Bible is to be believed, cannot be defined by these same scientific parameters . . .

For isn't this the holy dogma that the faithful theologians advocate as being undeniably true?

But what well-educated human being (who hasn't been indoctrinated into a religious dogma) . . .

Truly believes that God would be the one exception to so many scientific laws?

Yet, if a faithful believer is compelled to ignore such logic . . .

And does, in fact, fully accept that God exists without having had a beginning . . .

Then a corresponding question would be:

When a person professes such a belief in God's existence . . .

Is this religious conviction a function of their childhood indoctrination . . .

Or is such a belief based upon a rational understanding of the verifiable facts?

For if a person accepts the clergy's advocacy for the existence of God . . .

Then might not such a person also want to ask himself or herself, per the context of this inquiry, if it's probable that they would have such a belief . . .

If instead of having been born into a

religious family, they'd grown up in a non-religious household and had thus been taught (from an early age) to be highly skeptical of fanciful superstitions, i.e., . . .

If such a person's education had, instead, been based upon rational systems of thought in regards to analyzing a theological concept such as the existence of God?

For when a person has, in fact, been taught (from an early age) to believe in certain religious subjectivities and also has been indoctrinated into a system of theological dogma . . .

Then hasn't such a person's mind been conditioned to think in a religiously approved fashion . . .

Because such a person surely is aware of the fact that many times their answers to theological questions are not based upon the logic of scientific deduction; but are, instead, simply regurgitations of their childhood religious indoctrination?

Note also that the clergy, per this context, will (of course) strenuously defend their dogmatic point of view . . .

By emphasizing their superior theological understanding . . .

And state that such complex inquiries of faith are beyond the average person's ability to comprehend . . .

While referencing the opinion that the masses should avoid such metaphysical questions . . .

In that most people can only assimilate simplistic religious concepts and thus must rely upon the easy-to-understand religious doctrines taught by the clergy.

In other words, such troubling theological questions should not be asked at all.

But, of course, we strongly disagree . . .

Because questioning the motivations of those who directly benefit from an addictive thought philosophy is an honorable path. And if we can advocate such inquiries without repression, without the bullying label of heresy . . .

Without having inquisitors enforcing death sentences upon such skeptics (as has repeatedly occurred throughout the millennia) . . .

Then this is the freedom of expression that we seek. For how many courageous individuals, at the time of the Spanish Inquisition . . .

Had the fortitude to stand up and say what they believed to be true, i.e., . . .

Had the courage to defend the innocent from the mighty inquisitors . . .

Had the honesty to state that they believed that the Earth was round (and not flat) and that it rotated around the Sun and that diseases were caused by microorganisms and not demons?

Dare we forget the fundamental beginnings of the mainstream religions, e.g., their backward thinking and superstitious viewpoints . . .

And how these exact same core philosophies have continued . . .

Throughout the ages . . .

And still endure today?

Surely the enlightened among us know that the world's mainstream religions were not initially constructed as they presently exist . . .

For when these thought philosophies were first conceived and introduced to the masses . . .

The theologies of Judaism, Christianity, and Islam were all presented with less defined dogmas . . .

And only after an extended evolutionary process did they proceed to "evolve" from their initiating doctrines.

And doesn't this slow evolution of dogma, in and of itself, serve as yet another proof that such belief systems were first based (at their inception) . . .

Not upon divine intervention . . .

But upon superstitious falsehoods?

Specifically, if an all-knowing and all-powerful God had a true desire to transfer his "holy" message to the masses (in order to help humanity) . . .

Wouldn't logic dictate that such a God would've done so per a very accurate system of thought from the very inception of his divine communication and without a need for his holy message to be continually revised and updated . . .

At different points in the future . . .

For wouldn't an all-powerful supreme being have had the ability to be extremely precise and exact in communicating his "intent" to mankind? And surely an omnipotent God would have been able to transfer an easily understood message to all of mankind in one microsecond, would he not?

Then why didn't God do so?

Or, another way of asking the same question:

Why didn't God simply implant the required DNA in all of us so we could fully comply with his holy intent and thus avoid the tempting mistakes that the clergy has labeled as sins?

Furthermore, if God's intent was to truly help us, then why did he transfer different versions of his holy message in fits and starts over thousands of years?

Seems highly suspicious, does it not?

And remember, the mainstream religions have declared that it's impossible for God to make a mistake, have they not?

For isn't God absolutely perfect?

But wait. If this statement is, indeed, true; and if God is absolutely perfect, then why didn't he make sure that his (chosen) human messengers were capable of transferring his holy intent . . .

Without any miscommunication?

In other words, why have there been endless debates and reinterpretations as to what God's true message was (and is)?

And why would God have chosen to transfer his holy commands only to a very few individuals at diverse moments in time? Why wouldn't God have -- if his intent was to honestly help all of mankind -- why wouldn't he have instantly proclaimed his precise message to all tribes at the exact same moment in history?

Assuredly, these are questions that the clergy (of all faiths) cannot answer, can they? And the reason that they can't answer these momentous questions is because such "people of God" are nothing more than illegitimate purveyors of magical thinking. They are not, and have never been, the chosen messengers of a supreme being.

For, as most of us know, Christianity did not have a spontaneous beginning, in that it evolved from Judaism. Jesus Christ was a Jew; and Christ used his own interpretation of Judeo dogma . . .

To define his thought schism . . .

Because his rebel preachings branched off from Jewish orthodoxy, i.e., Jesus's Christianity began as a Jewish cult.

And even more intriguing -- if Christ's teachings were, indeed, factual (as they've been presented as being in the New Testament) . . .

Then why did his schism from Judaism (which evolved into the thought philosophy now known as Christianity) . . .

Why wasn't Christ's dogmatic ideology given to Moses by God when God initially transferred his holy message to his chosen people (i.e., the Jews)? In other words, the Roman Catholic Church fully believes that the Old Testament (the Hebrew Bible) was inspired by God; and the Church also accepts, without any doubt whatsoever, that Judaism was the initiating thought system that eventually evolved into Christianity . . .

But yet, how does the Church explain the inconsistency of why God didn't transfer his true "Christian" message to the early Hebrew prophets, i.e., why did God delay his holy intent . . .

In that God didn't offer Jesus's teachings to his "chosen people" at the inception of Judaism . . .

For it took thousands of years for the Christian messiah to finally arrive on Earth with God's "newly revealed" gospel, did it not?

So if God's intent was to truly help mankind as expeditiously as possible . . .

Then why didn't God give Moses his intended Christian message on Mt. Sinai?

Or why didn't God transfer his Christian intent to Noah before Noah built his ark?

Or why didn't God give his Christian message to Abraham?

But these holy transferences . . .

Didn't occur . . .

For if the Church's dogma is to be believed, God -- for some unknown reason -- delayed the conveyance of his true gospel.

IV

Why Has God Made So Many Mistakes?

For almost two thousand years, the clerics of the Christian Church have slowly constructed a 3-dimensional web of intricate rationalizations . . .

In order to explain the many illogical inconsistencies of their faith. And, in so doing, they've imprinted their religious dogma with a number of compelling psychological indoctrinations . . .

Which function to defend their superstitious thought system against debate . . .

And which have also been used to empower Christianity with a protective brainwashing that has the ability to counteract a variety of inquiries mounted by skeptical minds.

Of course Islam has also employed a

similar psychological technique in order to achieve the same effect. For example, when one analyzes the thought foundations of the Muslim faith, an intriguing question arises as to why the prophet Muhammad was compelled to assert the claim that his lineage traced all the way back to Abraham and the "people of the book" (i.e., the Jews).

Specifically, how did Muhammad know for a fact that he was related to Abraham? Was such documentation of Muhammad's genealogy available to him (or to anyone else for that matter) . . .

During the time that Muhammad actually lived . . .

Which was roughly six hundred years after Christ had died . . .

Or should Muslims simply accept on faith (and not reason) that God himself had to have told Muhammad that he was a direct descendent of Abraham?

Furthermore, why did God instruct Muhammad to generate yet another schism of God's ever-changing dogma? What possible reason would God have had for intentionally delaying his "true" holy message for such an extended amount of time?

Or could this delay have been because God had concluded that all of his previous attempts at communicating his holy commandments to the masses had, for some unknown reason, tragically failed; and so God decided to "evolve" Judaism and Christianity into yet another revised version of his heavenly intent, i.e., God wanted to offer the world yet another "true" religion . . .

Which came to be known as Muhammad's Islam?

But wait.

How could Judaism and Christianity have been inherently flawed . . .

And thus considered by God to have been failed religions . . .

If they'd truly been given to man by God?

Remember, God is perfect, is he not?

So why would God have intentionally delayed his "true" holy message in such a way, i.e., why, for thousands of years, did God postpone the transference of his divine intent?

But this did, in fact, transpire . . .

Did it not . . .

If we're to believe Muhammad's version of events?

Yet . . .

Conversely . . .

If God wanted the world to clearly understand his holy intent (going all the way back to Adam and/or Noah), then why did God intentionally postpone the transference of his Islamic dogma?

Any idea?

And here's yet another conundrum. If this is the first time that you've ever been presented with this hidden knowledge, then why has it taken so long for these religious inconsistencies to be clearly defined per a textual offering? Doesn't it seem a little odd that such questions haven't been debated in the media?

Indeed, why have such obvious flaws in the world's major religions been hidden from the masses for so long?

Any clue?

Now, of course, certain highly informed readers will be able to answer . . .

This question . . .

Yet, since there will also be many others who'll be unable to . . .

Because the answer isn't commonly known . . .

Then let us offer our opinion.

We believe that the mainstream religions have had no choice but to continually readjust their so-called holy dogmas so as to be able to evolve their "Godly" messages . . .

In order to be able to keep their fanciful superstitions relevant . . .

And thus consistent . . .

Per mankind's ever-increasing assimilation of scientific knowledge.

For clearly, throughout history, there's been a constant evolution of religious theology . . .

And such theological reconfigurations, in and of themselves, underscore the symptomatic inconsistencies of these magical philosophies . . .

In that when the shaman-clerics have had to repeatedly readjust their perception of God's intent so as to contemporize the believability of his holy dogma per the world's increased acceptance of scientific logic . . .

This constant theological restructuring places into question the legitimacy of the initiating holy commandments, does it not? In other words, for the clergy to have had to change and update God's divine message due to man's mental progression . . .

From illiterate primitive . . .

To scientific modern . . .

Such revisionisms of God's will, we believe, serve as clear evidence that the initiating holy dogmas were flawed from inception.

And so, per this application of evidentiary reasoning . . .

When mainstream religious doctrines are, in fact, objectively analyzed . . .

An enlightened understanding begins to take hold; and the clergy's hidden intent becomes evident . . .

And can thus be labeled for what it truly is.

Religious propaganda.

In a word, for the clergy to have had to constantly reconfigure God's holy message in order to keep it relevant . . .

Such intentional reconfigurations, if viewed objectively by a rational thinker, function as proof that the originating holy transferences . . .

Either weren't truthfully transcribed (because most of the Biblical events didn't actually occur) . . .

Or because such religious messages have been reworded and changed vis-à-vis a compelling need to keep them relevant . . .

Which means that the originating dogmas were nothing more than creative fictions . . .

Since they were, in fact, conceived of by inventive scribes and thus were not transferred to man by God . . .

Because the clergy has been compelled to have them rewritten . . .

Or, when viewed collectively, it means

that God never intended to transfer an everlasting divine message to mankind at all . . .

Even though the imams do fully believe that Muhammad's Koran is God's final attempt at offering the world a definitive holy dogma.

But if the imams are wrong and if we're correct in our thesis that there is no God, then we predict that there will be yet another reconfigured divine transference . . .

By yet another holy prophet at some point in the future . . .

Who will present to the masses . . .

Yet another spiritual doctrine . . .

And that this new prophet will then proceed to proclaim that his revised gospel was given to him by God and that it truly is God's ever-lasting dogma.

For assuredly, as has occurred with the thought manipulations of the shaman-clerics of the past, such a future transference will also have the same corresponding addictive qualities . . .

And thus will be, we believe, emblematic of humanity's craving for superstitious empowerments . . .

In that the human mind has a genetic vulnerability to magical thinking.

Ergo, we firmly believe that all religious dogmas . . .

Are nothing more . . .

Than fictional creations . . .

Which have been generated by rebellious individuals . . .

So as to increase their own worth.

And in this regard, it's instructive to note that such an opinion becomes clearly evident when an objective review of the historical record is undertaken . . .

And thus one is able to disregard the superstitious impingements . . .

Of Biblical myth . . .

Because it's unmistakably apparent that the founders of all of the mainstream religions . . .

Sought to attain a higher social status by replacing a prevailing . . .

Superstitious dogma . . .

With their reconfigured thought configurations . . .

And that their corresponding claims of communicating with God were nothing more than fanciful fabrications.

V

The Evolution of Addictive Theology

In the previous chapter, we stated that mainstream religions have had to continually revise their holy dogmas . . .

So as to keep them relevant per man's ever-increasing scientific understanding. Let's now examine how such dogmatic modifications did, in fact, evolve throughout history.

First, before the Hebrews formalized their belief system, they were thought to have migrated throughout the Middle East. And it also should be noted that it was via these extended migrations that the early Hebrews, as a union of tribes, began to assimilate various religious ideologies, which they eventually reformulated into Judaism.

Hence, the Hebrew philosophical concept of the existence of only one god . . .

Wasn't initiated per an instantaneous holy event . . .

But rather it evolved per the usurping of a variety of earlier religious dogmas . . .

Dogmas which were progressively reconfigured by the ancient Hebrews so as to empower their tribe with a much more addictive ideological formula than could be attained via polytheism.

So what actually occurred wasn't a miraculous event . . .

In that there wasn't an instantaneous assumption of monotheism . . .

But rather, there was a slow evolution of thought to a more focused and sustainable theology . . .

Which had the added ability of generating an addictive emotional response . . .

In that monotheism propagated an increased dependency . . .

On tribal indoctrination . . .

Via the repetition of empowering rituals, which functioned to energized the social will by generating a more intense focus on there only being "one' all-powerful god . . .

As opposed to having tribal initiates splitting their thought concentration between a multitude of deities (as had previously occurred with the preceding superstitious dogmas).

Specifically, the ancient Hebrews didn't transcribe a unique message from God, nor were their religious precepts totally original.

Far from it.

The early Hebrews simply assimilated a variety of thought ideologies from the preexisting religious cultures that they had come in contact with, and it was via this practical co-opting of addictive religious formulations . . .

Which gave the Jews the ability to eventually formalize their own monotheism and thus begin to coalesce their thought propaganda into a more unified tribal intent.

And though they were exceedingly successful . . .

At evolving their theology into a highly focused single-god thought system . . .

The resulting ideology wasn't achieved vis-à-vis their origination of a totally new religious philosophy . . .

But was, instead, nothing more than an evolved ideological formulation . . .

Which functioned to unify the tribal meme, in that . . .

Monotheism was simply a reconfiguration of preexisting pagan philosophies.

And it should also be noted that the word "meme" -- in this context -- is defined as a thought virus which can be transferred from person to person and which has the addictive ability to replicate per an ever-changing pattern. Specifically, thought memes resemble social fads . . .

In that they can become embedded in a person's consciousness.

For example, the first time a young child sees a teenager riding a bicycle, the young child may begin to fixate on acquiring his own bicycle . . .

Then once the young child has a bicycle, he may see yet another teenager riding a motorcycle, and thus the young child begins to fixate on acquiring his own motorcycle.

To further clarify, we believe that certain obsessive thoughts are processed by our brains somewhat like addictive substances. Consequently, when habitual thought systems are continually refined and distilled into purer forms by the shaman-clerics . . .

In order to attain a higher theological potency . . .

Then the masses can (and do) become addicted to these narco-dogmas.

Hence, religions are the ultimate social addiction, in that, throughout history, such superstitious ideologies have caused the codependent deaths of millions of people . . .

Per a never-ending series of religious conflicts . . .

For, unfortunately, there's been a constant warring over which Biblical philosophy is truly correct . . .

Over which tribe has the ear of God . . .

In that such mass-ego indoctrinations have been exceptionally tragic (and are quite similar in scope to prodigious drug addictions) . . .

And will continue to be socially destructive until mankind is able to one day kick its superstitious dependency . . .

And thus recognize its debilitating God addiction for what it truly is.

But we digress. Getting back to the evolution of Judeo dogma . . .

The ancient Hebrews were able to reconfigure their belief system into the highly addictive theology of monotheism . . .

Which proceeded to energize their faithful via focusing their collective thoughts on only one god . . .

But this ideological configuration did not purge the Hebrews of all pagan superstitions . . .

For they continued to advocate animal sacrifices and also persisted with the invocation of magical phrases so as to bring blessings upon themselves and harm unto their enemies.

And it should also be noted that a number of Biblical scholars are of the opinion that Zoroastrianism and the Egyptian pharaoh-cult of Akhenaten . . .

Were actually the first truly monotheistic religions, in that both of these seminal dogmas preceded the formalization of the Hebrew's monotheism.

To further clarify -- numerous Pharaoh cults had, in fact, existed in Egypt long before the Hebrews wrote their Torah. And even though most Biblical scholars are of the opinion that the early Hebrews did not share a common lineage with the Egyptians -- the Hebrews . . .

(Having migrated into Egypt) . . .

Began to assimilate certain parts of the Pharaoh's belief system into Judaism (as did the Christians at a later point in time). Isis and her son Horus (two Egyptian gods) were integrated into the Jewish and Christian Bibles, albeit with different names.

Now, instructionally, it's important to understand why the Hebrews were compelled to adopt certain elements of the Pharaoh's religion . . .

Since this belief acquisition involved a sacred foundation of Judaism (and

Christianity) . . .

In that this Egyptian-thought assimilation precipitated the Biblical story of the infant Moses being set adrift down the Nile.

For, if the truth be known, Moses's Biblical childhood was nothing more than a fanciful myth that was stolen from the pagans. The Jewish infant-down-the-Nile story, as written in the Bible, was simply a manufactured plot device . . .

Which was designed to function as a "holy pedigree" for the Hebrew prophet. Moses's childhood (as described in the Bible) was, in actuality, nothing more than a plagiarized storytelling device that hadn't been based upon any factual events -- in that this fictionalized storyline was creatively generated by the Hebrew storytellers because it served to establish a much needed emotional bond to the faithful . . .

In that this infant-in-danger myth was chosen because it would instantly connect the Hebrew's most important prophet to the masses via emotional sympathy.

Indeed, who would be so coldhearted as to not have compassion for a person who had been set adrift down the mighty Nile as a little baby?

And, to further clarify, the Hebrew storytellers weren't, in fact, the originators of this infant-down-the-Nile myth . . .

Since this sympathetic device almost exactly mimics the earlier "pagan" myth about Horus . . .

In that the Egyptian god Horus had been emotionally enhanced with a similar childhood "pedigree" . . .

And, of course, this compelling religious "pedigree" was originated . . .

Not via Hebrew dogma, but via a pre-existing Egyptian dogma . . .

In that it had been a well-established pagan myth . . .

Which claimed that the infant Horus had been hidden in the Nile's marshland long before the Biblical account of Moses was propagandized by the Hebrews.

So, per this context, the childhood ascribed to Moses is nothing more than a "pagan" myth . . .

And is not a Biblical truth, i.e., . . .

Moses's childhood is clearly a religious fairy tale (if you will) that was plagiarized from the Egyptians.

Thereupon, this Biblical falsification brings up a telling insight. For if the Hebrew scribes (who wrote the Old Testament) had no qualms about fictionalizing Moses's childhood (a prophet whom they claimed to have spoken to God) . . .

Then what does this mean?
Does it mean that . . .

If parts of the Old and New Testaments were, indeed, fabricated from earlier pagan belief systems . . .

Then, based upon this truth, the scribes who generated the so-called holy messages of the Bible weren't actually bound by truth when they put pen to parchment?

In other words, when such a forensic analysis of the textual record is taken into consideration -- it becomes clear that the Hebrew storytellers (who generated the Old Testament) . . .

Weren't at all constrained by a code of honesty, nor were they compelled to truthfully describe the actual facts of the Biblical events . . .

When they wrote their addictive religious commentary . . .

For doesn't the plagiarized religious "pedigree" which the Hebrew scribes used to elevate Moses's status . . .

Prove that these early storytellers did, in fact, employ fictionalized enhancements?

And, in this regard, it seems quite obvious that this "paganization" was employed so as to emotionalize (and dramatize) the newly created holy dogma . . .

Because such an amplification technique

had already been proven to be highly effective in generating an addictive religious myth . . .

A myth that had empowered the Pharaoh's mind control. For clearly, the Hebrew storytellers wanted to elevate Moses's status . . .

(Their most important prophet) . . .

And thus they chose to do so by embellishing his childhood via copying certain parts of a pagan god story from the Egyptians.

Therein -- in order to establish their own "holy" legitimacy (so to speak), the ancient Hebrews were compelled to characterize their hero-prophet Moses . . .

As having had . . .

An auspicious childhood . . .

Mimicking Pharaoh's highly effective religious propaganda . . .

And thus the Hebrews employed this proven "pedigree" technique, which had been so successfully utilized by the Egyptians . . .

To emotionally elevate the Egyptian god Horus.

And here it should also be noted that when storytellers, in general, take on the task of generating new fiction (or new gospel) . . .

It's much easier to repeat a previously created myth from an earlier source . . .

Than to have to completely create a totally new and emotionally compelling dramatic plotline vis-à-vis their own imaginations.

Remember, someone had to write the Bible. It wasn't written by the hand of God. Also, if one accepts our assertion that the Bible wasn't inspired by God; but was, instead, creatively imagined by a group of magical thinkers who proceeded to blend fact with fiction . . .

Then one can begin to understand why the various scribes who actually wrote the Bible had been tribally motivated to do so by employing such dramatic techniques. Specifically, they wanted their "holy" chronicle to be as readable and addictive as possible; and in order to achieve this goal, they used various literary mechanisms so as to enhance their captivating dogma.

So, per this textual assessment, the Biblical scribes were not and did not have the intent of being honest documentarians of historical facts. Their craft technique of employing fictional enhancements, i.e., . . .

Of plagiarizing . . .

Pagan systems of thought . . .

Clearly calls into question the

verisimilitude of the Holy Bible.

Note also that Moses was portrayed as having god-like abilities, in that he was characterized as having supernatural powers. But when we again apply an objective analysis in order to discern the implied literary intent, such a story enhancement opens an important window into understanding the mindset of the storytellers who felt compelled to insert such a character trait into the Biblical record.

And, therein, it's per this analysis of intent . . .

That leads us to conclude that such heroic enhancements in the Bible were, in fact, subtextual pagan echoes, in that even though the Hebrew scribes were attempting to promote Yahweh as being the one-and-only god per claiming that he was more powerful than the Egyptian gods associated with Pharaoh . . .

(And more powerful than Pharaoh as a living god) . . .

The Hebrew clerics, via their mimicking imaginations, continued to mirror pagan dogma. In other words, the Hebrew scribes were compelled to create a fictionalized heroic Jew . . .

Who proceeded to function somewhat like a god, in that Moses was able to bring plagues down upon the Egyptians and part the Red Sea and turn his staff into a serpent.

In sum, Moses was depicted as having the supernatural abilities of a pagan god.

So the ideological war between slave and master . . .

Became a war . . .

Of the imaginations, i.e., . . .

Became a propaganda feud over whose god was mightier, over which tribe could generate the most addictive thought philosophy.

And even though the Hebrews had "begun to believe" in only one God, Moses became Yahweh's god surrogate, if you will, in that Moses was portrayed as functioning somewhat like a god-figure stand-in per his fictionalized supernatural abilities to avenge the enemies of the Jews (i.e., the enslaving Egyptians).

And, of course, a similar god-enhancing technique also reoccurred when the Christian scribes later penned Jesus's persona . . .

In that those subsequent Biblical writers also mirrored their pagan roots by giving Christ the "pedigree" of an auspicious virgin birth and thus the ability to perform supernatural feats (e.g., of raising the dead, turning water into wine, healing the sick, and reenergizing his own spirit after he'd been crucified).

But again, such holy enhancements weren't unique (or original) to either the Jews or the Christians . . .

Because the Biblical childhoods of Moses and Jesus were, in fact . . .

Plagiarized fictions . . .

Which closely mimicked the earlier pagan myth generated by Pharaoh's scribes. For both of these religious "pedigrees" were copied from the Egyptian dogma . . .

Which claimed that the Pharaoh god Osiris had impregnated the "virgin" Isis . . .

Who then gave birth to . . .

The god Horus . . .

Who was then set adrift down the Nile.

Sound familiar?

Hence, when one investigates the historical facts, it becomes clear that the Hebrew and Christian scribes simply reconfigured an ancient Egyptian myth of the virgin-mother Isis (a.k.a., the Virgin Mary) and her son Horus (a.k.a., Moses/Jesus).

Plus, it should also be noted, in regards to Christ's childhood . . .

What is strangely missing from the New Testament . . .

Also functions as a critical clue as to the

historical truthfulness of that Biblical account.

For clearly -- if Jesus Christ was God's son, then why did he live in relative obscurity until the latter years of his life? For if Jesus was, in fact, a human god from birth (being as Christian dogma states that his mother, Mary, knew that she'd been a virgin at conception . . .

And also was well aware that God had miraculously placed Jesus in her womb) . . .

Then wouldn't it seem logical that Christ's childhood and young adult years would've been highly eventful, instead of being so anonymous and obscure?

Indeed, how could such a god-like human have lived such a relatively normal life for almost 30 years? And how was the secret of Christ's divinity kept hidden from his village?

Furthermore, why isn't there a Biblical record of anyone, anyone at all, interacting with Christ as a holy figure (i.e., as the son of God) -- except when he was first born and then only much later, per the final few years of his life?

Moreover, if the Gospel of Matthew is to be believed, didn't three wise men from the east (i.e., the Magi, a.k.a., the Zoroastrians) come looking for the newborn King of the

Jews? Plus, wasn't Herod documented in the Bible as having committed infanticide (the Massacre of the Innocents) . . .

So as to prevent the Jews from having a rebel king?

But yet, per the published Biblical record, is there any logic to Jesus having lived such an uneventful life . . .

As that of a lowly carpenter . . .

Or for the holy Messiah to have had such a relatively obscure life up until his baptism by John the Baptist . . .

If Jesus truly had such an auspicious virgin birth?

In other words, wouldn't such a notable person (i.e., a human god) . . .

Have had a moral obligation to minister God's intent long before he turned 30 years of age and was baptized by John? And remember, at that time in history, few people lived to be much older than forty years of age, did they not?

Or could this be yet another case of hidden knowledge, in that the Jew known as Jesus Christ . . .

Wasn't the Son of God at all? Instead, Jesus was simply a charismatic carpenter who had had a life-changing epiphany soon after being baptized by an angry rebel . . .

In that it was Christ's jarring immersion

in the River Jordan . . .

Which energized within him an overwhelming desire to revolt against the injustice of the status quo (i.e., his baptism became a psychological tipping point) . . .

But yet -- before his epiphanous rebirth from the murky water, Jesus had never actually considered himself to be the Son of God, nor had anyone else ascribed divine characteristics to his personality until after his death. For clearly, Christ's holy elevation occurred, not because he was the Messiah, but because . . .

The Christian scribes (tasked with generating a "pedigree" myth) . . .

Wanted to create their own addictive propaganda in response to the unjust crucifixion of their cult leader.

And so it was only after his rebellious crucifixion (and the subsequent propagandizing of his imagined "holy pedigree") . . .

That the Jesus-divinity myth began to coalesce into dogma. But during the time that Jesus actually lived, his insurgent actions mainly served as a political magnetic to other Hebrew rebels and, consequently, garnered the attention of the Roman overlords who, wanting to repress an uprising in their Hebrew colony, had Jesus crucified for sedition.

Therein, it was Christ's acolytes, not God, who wanted to preserve Jesus's defiant ministry . . .

And thus it was his acolytes who then proceeded to propagandize his biography via giving him a "god-like pedigree" so as to elevate his divine status and thereupon generate a mass appeal for a reconfigured Jewish cult . . .

Which eventually became known as Christianity.

Of course -- Muhammad's persona was similarly enhanced by his followers . . .

But, of course . . .

To a much lesser extent . . .

For Muhammad's ascension into heaven at the Dome of the Rock, per Islamic dogma, could also be viewed as yet another example of an angry rebel being spiritually enhanced, ex post factor, via a fictionalized god-like ability.

In sum -- we believe that the many scribes who wrote the various chapters of the Bible weren't transcribing God's unique message, nor were they hearing the voice of God.

No, not at all.

They were simply talented storytellers endowed with highly creative imaginations, and they proceeded to transcribe their own inner voices, not the voice of God . . .

For this is what fiction writers do.

And because, through the ages, the masses have been kept in the dark as to how such religious dogmas were actually conceived and written . . .

This means that a vast majority of the religious faithful has also been excluded from understanding how truly easy it was for the initiating Biblical writers to manufacture such fictions . . .

Vis-à-vis plagiarizing them from pagan myths . . .

And then elevating these myths into religious dogma per being blended with historical events.

And since at the time that the Bible was actually written, there were no copyright laws or strict taboos against such plagiarizations . . .

Stealing from preexisting sources was fairly common.

Nevertheless -- most of today's religious faithful are of the mindset that the Bible was written and codified per a "sacred" standard. Yet all of the naive souls who've been taught this, i.e., . . .

Taught that the Bible was written with extraordinary integrity . . .

Do not take into account that our

modern-day modes of documentation and fact-checking did not exist in those ancient times. Today's faithful are ignoring the true reality of what really happened per the Bible's lengthy creation, and few even consider the possibility . . .

That there were various political intrigues and tribal agendas at play . . .

Besides an adherence to absolute honesty and truthfulness . . .

In regards to the scribes who actually wrote the various books of the Judeo-Christian Bible.

And what is also troubling is why the faithful believers of today fully assume that the formulators of the Biblical record were motivated by good intentions?

Specifically, what historical document actually proves this assumption to be an uncontestable fact? Have any biographies of the actual authors of the Bible ever been published? Do we even know if these so-called "holy" scribes were considered to be of honest character by their fellow villagers?

No, we do not.

Nor do we know what other religious texts (or non-religious documents) . . .

The Biblical scribes may've penned (at an earlier date) before they actually sat down to write the Bible. For wouldn't common logic imply that such elite writers would've surely begun their writing careers via penning earlier texts as opposed to beginning their profession by first documenting a book inspired by God?

For surely the task of writing a chapter in the Torah or New Testament would have been preceded by numerous other writing assignments, in that these holy writers must have written earlier preliminary documents before they ever began working on their Biblical entries.

Also, here's yet another intriguing question.

What were the backgrounds of the holy storytellers who initially passed along the pre-textual oral histories (i.e., the originating verbal stories), which were only later written down by the Hebrew and Christian scribes?

Indeed, who were these people who claimed that their Biblical stories were absolutely true; and what were their motivations; and did any of these ancient storytellers have criminal backgrounds?

But, of course, no one can answer these troubling questions, can they? The Biblical record is void . . .

Of such forensic discernments . . .
Void of such salient details . . .

Details, which have yet to be explained by the clergy.

Of course a smug scholar might dismiss such inquiries with the common assumption that only a well-educated citizen functioned as a scribe at the time that the first Biblical stories were thought to have been written down. For truly, everyone knows that the average citizen of those distant times didn't know how to write (or even read) . . .

Because at that moment in history (when the Bible was initially formulated) -- any form of writing would've been a highly specialized endeavor, would it have not?

Hence, per such scholarly thinking, the assumption is that the Bible was, in all probability, documented by a select group of elite scribes who must have been of good character.

But is this truly a verifiable fact, or is this yet another convenient assumption?

In today's world, we only have to check the police blotter to become aware of the fact that a number of highly educated citizens are flawed with criminal intent. For not only have politicians and corporate leaders been prosecuted for transgressing into corruption (per the greed of money and power) . . .

But various clergymen have also been

taken to court for numerous crimes. Have not there been hundreds of child molestations by Catholic priests, Protestant ministers, and Jewish rabbis?

And so to naively assume that the early Hebrew scribes were somehow excluded from flawed intent . . .

Is bogus.

The skill set needed to write words on a page does not implicitly imply honesty or grant such authors the validity of good character. Writers are as flawed as all individuals. And remember, there were no federal certifications and no copyright standards in regards to truth telling in ancient times. There was no book police to verify the truthfulness of the early Hebrew-Christian-Islamic scribes.

VI

Where Did God Actually Come From?

In order to clarify the thought evolution from paganism to monotheism . . .

There is yet another facet of hidden knowledge that should be explored. And to do this, we will begin by asking:

Does the concept of there being just one God make any sense at all?

Think about it. In nature is there ever just one of anything?

So, per this context . . .

If the belief in only one god is to have any logic to it whatsoever . . .

Would not this also mean that God doesn't have to conform to the natural laws of the universe . . .

Since, via the cosmology of the infinite, there never is just one of anything, is there?

Is there only one planet in the universe?
No.
Is there only one koala bear?
No.
Is there only one redwood tree?
No.
Is there only one glacier?
No.

And furthermore, why is this universal truth so categorically broad in its reality? In other words, why does there always appear to be a multiple of everything in the universe?

Could the answer be because it is totally illogical and unnatural for there to be only one of anything? Could the laws of nature actually prevent the existence of only one "form of matter" from occurring?

Hence, if true -- then, per reasoned logic, the concept of monotheism appears to be highly flawed, in that such a concept doesn't reflect the laws of science as we presently understand them.

And so, per this rational objectivity, what does the concept of there only being one god truly mean?

If it means that God has no peers, no community of gods, and no parents . . .

If it means that the one true God is singular . . .

Then a corollary question arises as to where did God, in fact, come from.

The theologians would have us believe that God is infinite and that he has "always been and will always be."

Yet -- if viewed objectively -- is this concept at all logical, or could this simply be yet another religious rationalization that's been conveniently designed to explain the unexplainable?

For when the originators of the Christian Church established their dogma of the Holy Trinity and proclaimed that there was only one true God (the Holy Father) and Jesus Christ (God's son) and the Holy Ghost (?) . . .

Wasn't the creation of this divine dogma simply an echo from the pagan past . . .

For couldn't a nonreligious observer consider the Holy Trinity to be nothing more than a mythic reverberation of the belief in a multiple of gods? In other words, isn't the Holy Trinity . . .

Yet another way to explain how Jesus Christ could have been godlike, yet not actually be God himself, per se, since there is but one god?

A conundrum of sorts, is it not?

But if Christian dogma is to be believed,

then Jesus Christ was the "son" of God. However, why did God have to have . . .

A son . . .

And is this, in fact, truly monotheism; or is this, in actuality, evolved polytheism?

Now, of course, the Christian clergy will answer such a question by stating that God sent his "only begotten son" down to Earth in order for Jesus to serve as a divine go-between (so to speak), i.e., . . .

In order for Christ to be able to bring God's message to humanity via Jesus being able to experience a humanly existence.

But wait. Why did God need his son to become partially human in order for God's message to be fully applied?

Or maybe this had nothing to do . . .

With God . . .

Maybe this dogma was advocated because the Christian clergy, in order to keep their flawed illusion viable, was compelled to satisfy the emotional needs of their faithful by having them believe that Jesus (and thus God) was somehow better able to understand our humanness . . .

But which, in and of itself, actually achieved the reverse effect . . .

In that this son-of-God dogma served to humanize the god-force and thus make it more accessible, i.e., . . .

More humanly relatable . . .

To the faithful . . .

By having such a powerful god manifest himself into a god-human form.

In other words, by assuming a human existence, did this give the Messiah the anthropomorphic experience that he needed in order to better understand mankind . . .

Since such an experiential comprehension would not have occurred if Jesus had only maintained his godly form . . .

Or was this god-human dogma simply employed because it intensified the faithful's addiction to a manufactured superstition?

But there is yet another nagging perplexity to this theological conundrum . . .

Because if God is all-knowing . . .

Then why would he need to generate a son so as to be able to experience human existence? Indeed, would not God already know all there is to know about human emotion?

Hence, per this line of reasoning, does the doctrine of the Holy Trinity appear to be a logical reality . . .

Or is it yet another convenient theological rationalization that's been generated by the Christian shaman-clerics so as to explain the unexplainable?

Of course, as is quite obvious from reading this text, we believe that the Bible is, without a doubt, nothing more than a compilation of mythic stories . . .

And not a holy revelation from an omniscient god . . .

Which means that the Holy Trinity is simply a flawed fiction, i.e., this doctrine is, in fact, a fanciful myth that was created to mitigate the many inconsistencies of Christian dogma . . .

Because, subsequent to its dispersal, in order to rationalize their God-Jesus doctrine, the Christian Church attempted to clarify their polytheistic roots by stating that all three "entities" of the Trinity were simply different forms of the same God.

Therein . . .

In order to frame their polytheism within a monotheistic provenance . . .

The Christian theologians conceived of the premise that there couldn't be more than one god . . .

Yet still there also had to exist three variations of the same God, i.e., the Holy Trinity.

But wait. Isn't that what the Hindus say about their gods? In the Hindu religion, isn't there but only one god-force, which has many faces?

So, in this regard, maybe Christian monotheism isn't true monotheism . . .

But rather it's a variant known as henotheism?

In any event -- in order to explain Christ's existence, the Christian clergy needed a dogma that would clarify God's desire to generate a son . . .

And, in so doing, the mythic storytellers were motivated to weave in a believable plot that would give God a compelling reason to have sent "his only begotten son" . . .

To Earth . . .

And thus they gave Jesus Christ the ultimate holy pedigree.

Consequently, "the-son-of-God" myth was generated . . .

Because it had the unique ability to bond Jesus (a Hebrew rebel) to the masses with a remarkable emotional power.

But wait. If there truly is but one god and if this god is, in fact, a singular entity with no family relationships . . .

To other gods . . .

Then why is there a need for this one-of-a-kind supreme being to reach out with a human son in order for him to be able to "relate" to human needs?

Of course there's yet another possible reason that this occurred . . .

In that it was due to the fact that the clergy needed a compelling psychological mechanism, which had the inherent emotional power to addict the masses to their imagined myth.

But if this is, in fact, true -- then regardless of its proven effectiveness as an addictive theology, the actual logic behind such a Trinity myth is nonexistent . . .

For why would God have needed an emotional bridge to his human creation? Wouldn't God already have had the required emotional understanding since he's an all-knowing and omnipotent supreme being?

So, per this telling example of flawed theology, it becomes obvious that the 3-dimensional web of Christian dogma, which has been advocated for almost two thousand years . . .

Can serve as proof, in and of itself, that God does not exist. For if God did exist, then his omnipresent power would have had no need whatsoever for such human intrigues. Having to weave such complex explanations in order to explain away the many illogical inconsistencies of faith . . .

Confirms that the masses have been repeatedly deceived by the superstitions of magical thinking . . .

For if there is a God and if his intent is

to transfer a holy revelation to mankind . . .

Then such a god could have easily done so in an instant. And all of the religious rationales for him not taking such action are simply creative fictions that have been imagined by those seeking power and control over others.

Nothing more, nothing less.

And the sooner the world accepts the truth of this hidden knowledge . . .

The sooner we will evolve from superstitious primitives . . .

Forever addicted to magical thinking . . .

Into truly enlightened human beings.

VII

Why Would an Omniscient God Need Anyone to Pray to Him?

Having examined mainstream religion's evolution . . .
    From ancient superstitions . . .
    To modern dogma . . .
We now shift our inquiry to yet another falsehood of magical thinking.
    Prayer.
    Now . . .
    Quite probably . . .
Most people reading this text will have never questioned why so many religions advocate prayer . . .
    Or pondered . . .
Why the faithful (through the ages) have been taught that they must pray in order to prove their loyalty to God . . .

Hoping to gain his favor.

But think about it. Why would an all-knowing God need anyone to pray to him? If God is truly omniscient . . .

Then why would there be any reason at all to communicate the particulars of a person's life to God via prayer?

Wouldn't God already know when someone is sick . . .

Or when someone has sinned and wants to be forgiven?

So . . .

Why would God need humans to pray to him? It makes no sense. An all-knowing God would already be aware of all that there is to know, would he not? God would not actually need informative prayers . . .

In order for him to make a decision as to what to do about whatever.

But wait. Maybe prayer is simply a way for the faithful to show respect for God.

Could this be true?

Yet -- why would such a reason have any validity? Would not God also already know the truth as to whom does, in fact, respect him as compared to those who are simply going through the motions of acting as though they believe in his holy power but really do not?

Would not God already be cognizant of

such details?

So . . .

If prayer isn't something that's actually needed by God, then maybe it's a "false hope" that the faithful have been duped into believing. Maybe prayer has nothing to do with God. Maybe prayer is simply a conditioning process, which bonds believers to a religious ideology.

Could this be the true reason why the clergy demands that we pray to God?

In other words, is it logical, when someone commits a so-called sin . . .

For them to pray and admit that they have sinned and thus ask for forgiveness . . .

Hoping God will forgive them for their sinful action?

Is this the logic behind prayer?

Seems a little suspicious, does it not? For why would God demand that we follow his commandments . . .

Against certain actions . . .

But then allow for exceptions, adjusting his holy rules so as to compensate for our weaknesses . . .

In that God would be willing to overlook certain sins simply because someone did something so easy as praying?

Does this supposition have merit?

Here's a clue.

Is prayer hard to perform?

Does praying require any sacrifice at all?

And isn't it also true that absolutely anyone (mentally capable) can pray to God and "ask" for whatever they desire (knowing full well that their request may never be fulfilled)?

Of course, a number of religions have taboos as to what should or should not be prayed for . . .

Yet these admonishments do not actually prevent people from praying for whatever they want, do they?

Indeed, a murderer can pray and ask God for his crime to go unpunished, can he not?

And a corporate CEO can pray and ask God to increase her stock options, can she not?

Or what about a terrorist? Can't a terrorist pray to God and ask for a cache of high-powered explosives?

So -- when one investigates this so-called "religious" communication with God, one finds that the actual process of praying has little to do with good deeds or with the qualifications of those who are truly deserving . . .

Of God's intercession.

In other words, it is clear that the act of praying does not grant a participant any moral status at all. And even though most people may consider prayer to have a righteous foundation . . .

This linking of prayer to God has no factual basis in reality. The implied morality of prayer . . .

Has simply been embedded in the minds of the faithful per the addictive thought conditioning of religious dogma . . .

For there is no logic to prayer at all (other than the stress-relieving benefits of its meditative qualities).

Consider this. What does God do when thousands and thousands of people pray for contradictory outcomes? Does God sort through this flood of requests and select his favorites to fulfill? During wartime, does God only listen to the prayers of the American troops and ignore the heartfelt requests of the opposing forces?

And what about the desperate poor who live in Third World countries? Does God listen to their prayers? Does anyone truly believe that the starving children (in poor countries) . . .

Have done something to offend God when their prayers go unanswered?

And yet . . .

The poverty (in such countries) continues year after year . . .

Regardless of the prayers for God to intercede, does it not?

So, could teaching people to pray be nothing more than a propaganda tool employed by the clergy? Or, to put it another way, does the ritual of praying function as an addictive mechanism, i.e., does prayer somehow strengthen a believer's emotional bond to a religious dogma?

Of course, when investigating such an issue, the correct explanation may not be obvious . . .

Although it may appear to be quite obvious once the truth has been established.

For, at its basic level, silent prayer is simply another form of meditation . . .

And meditation is but another form of silent prayer. In both instances, a participant generates thoughts, which do not have to be verbalized. Also, with many forms of meditation, the purpose is to calm the mind and disconnect from the stress of everyday life.

For instance, some people may silently repeat a mantra over and over again. Others may visualize calming images. And though these meditative techniques may vary, the mantras used by certain religious sects can, in fact, be categorized as forms of prayer, in that a number of Eastern religions teach their believers to repeat certain words or phrases in order to attain a higher state of consciousness.

Plus, it should also be noted that medical science has validated the stress-relieving benefits of silent meditations. And, per alternative medicine, some Western doctors even prescribe meditation to their patients as a way to counterbalance an overactive mind.

So, in this regard, medical research has, in fact, confirmed the healing benefits of prayer.

Also, it should be noted that when Muslims are called to prayer or when Christians recite the Lord's Prayer . . .

(Over and over again) . . .

Or when Jews repeat the Torah . . .

A similar "healing" benefit can be achieved. Silent prayer and silent mediation are nothing more than different labels for the exact same calming mechanism.

Plus, it is also true that legitimate scientific research has confirmed that a certain percentage of ill patients have received a rejuvenating benefit from having other people pray for them.

And, of course, as would be expected, the

religious faithful have proceeded to claim that these documented medical cases serve as scientific proof for the healing power of prayer, in that it is their opinion that such research validates (without a doubt) that God does, in fact, exist.

But we disagree . . .

For there is no actual scientific proof that inserting the word . . .

"God" . . .

In a prayer or in a meditation (i.e., invoking God's name) . . .

Has anything whatsoever to do with the beneficial effects of prayer, other than the word itself functioning as a self-hypnosis empowerment. Indeed, we are of the opinion that praying with or without referring to God will work equally as well.

So -- when one garners a slight healing effect via prayer, this does not actually confirm the existence of God. The same medical benefits can also occur when nonbelievers pray without invoking God. People can pray and invoke themselves or invoke a fictional character from a comic book and still achieve the same healing effect . . .

If they truly believe without a doubt in their own self-hypnosis.

Furthermore, if a cult of seagull

believers invokes their bird god, and then their flock of birds proceeds to lay more eggs, does this prove (without a doubt) that their bird god exists?

Of course not.

What's at work here is an unexplained phenomenon which, we believe, is connected to the healing rewards of meditation . . .

And, therein . . .

Involves energizing the self-fulfilling power of group-thought (when such an effort focuses on a sick individual) . . .

Than any verification of the provability of the healing benefits of "Godly" prayer . . .

Which the religious faithful want to believe is irrefutable evidence that God does, in fact, exist.

For it is our opinion that science will eventually be able to logically explain the molecular mechanisms that are assisting such medical rejuvenations . . .

Because there are many mysteries of nature which science has not, as of yet, been able to clearly define. And even though certain people may have a snobby attitude as to what they think they know . . .

Such people tend to be remise . . .

In acknowledging that in every preceding age . . .

The conventional thinkers have always

assumed that they were absolutely correct in regards to similar issues . . .

Yet, historically, such thinking has repeatedly been proven wrong. For, in the past, when the world's educated elite had no doubt whatsoever that the world was flat and also believed that demons caused illnesses . . .

These concepts were wrongly deemed to be absolutely undeniable in their day and age.

So, in this regard, it is possible that there may be an unknown unification of existence, which has nothing to do with the religious definition of God, per se . . .

Although some have defined the word "God" to include such thinking, in that there are those who believe that all life is embodied within God . . .

And that nature, in and of itself, is a god-force (of sorts), and that the whole universe is, indeed, the cosmic body of God.

But obviously, to debate this consideration would involve a divergence from our focus (via this text) . . .

In that . . .

Such a tangent would incite an impractical philosophical debate as opposed to being a factual perception of reality . . .

And thus . . .

This expansion of thought falls outside of the boundaries of our intended inquiry . . .

For our intent here is not to debate the thought definitions of metaphysical possibilities . . .

But rather to focus on the superstitious propaganda of false realities.

VIII

Did God Create the Devil, or Did the Devil Create God?

As many know, dualism is the concept of God functioning in an antagonistic system of good versus evil.
    Dualism is also a thought meme . . .
    Which allows the faithful to believe that God is a loving deity who opposes the evil Devil.
    Now, of course, when such theological reasoning is objectively analyzed . . .
    An obvious flaw becomes evident.
    Specifically . . .
    Why would a compassionate creator (who is all-knowing and all-powerful) . . .
    Create an evil force to oppose him?
    It makes no sense . . .
    Because . . .

There is no logical reason for an omnipotent deity to intentionally create an extremely harmful adversary.

So why would a loving God create the evil of the Devil? Logic dictates that such a divine action would be inconceivable.

Hence, it's our opinion that the theology of dualism is clearly nothing more than a primitive superstition . . .

Because there would be no logical reason for God to embody an evil consciousness within a fallen angel such as the Devil. This belief that a personified evil exists is but another fanciful myth that's been embellished by the clergy.

Nevertheless, an interesting question does arise in regards to why the clergy had a desire to create such a mythic evil. Specifically, what motivated the thought initiators to conceive of the Devil? Or, to pose the question slightly differently:

How did the Biblical magical thinkers benefit from fictionalizing an opposing villain to their hero god?

And to understand why such a question needs to be asked, let's clarify the specifics.

First, there's the issue of the "conflict of opposites" . . .

In which a loving God controls one side of life's equation . . .

And the other side is controlled by the Devil (i.e., the personification of evil) who opposes God.

Of course, man is caught in the middle between these two forces . . .

Between the hero and the villain.

Sound familiar . . .

For isn't such a "conflict of opposites" . . .

Simply a classical storytelling technique? Or, to rephrase it:

Isn't such a well-crafted struggle between a good guy and a bad guy . . .

The most common dramatic structure used by writers to convey . . .

A compelling story . . .

In that almost all great stories use such a hero-villain plotting device to engage an audience, do they not?

In other words, haven't the best dramatists of the world (going all the way back to the Greeks and Aristotle) . . .

Used this device to engage their audiences with stories of good versus evil, with stories of heroes versus villains, with plotlines of protagonists versus antagonists?

For clearly, the "conflict of opposites" is, in fact, the most effective storytelling structure that a writer can employ if he wants to create a highly engaging plotline.

Hence, almost all great stage plays,

movies, and novels . . .

Employ a "conflict of opposites" where a heroic persona is opposed by a villainous antagonist . . .

For one only has to review a list of the highest rated stories of the last 4000 years to conclude that demonizing "the opposition" is a standard literary technique. In fact, this dramatic device can be traced all the way back to the earliest storytellers. The insightful Greek philosopher Aristotle even formalized such a theory in his book *Poetics* (which was written over 2000 years ago).

So there's an extensive historical precedence for authors writing dualistic stories. Employing such a dramatic tool . . .

Drives a story's plot forward and sharpens its emotional focus . . .

Because . . .

If a writer wants to heighten the emotional bond of a text, there's an inherent need to have at least two opposing characterizations in any great story.

Therein, when theologians reference thought systems where a god is in opposition to an evil antagonist . . .

This addictive dogma resonates with the suspicion of fictional invention.

In a word, we have no doubt that the scribes who compiled the Biblical stories did so by combining fanciful fiction (both plagiarized and original) . . .

With oral histories . . .

Of tribal empowerment . . .

And they then proceeded to edit these fictions into a Biblical presentation. Of course it's also quite understandable why these mythic storytellers chose to use such a highly effective literary tool as that of having their hero god be in opposition to an evil character such as a fallen angel, i.e., the Devil.

For without the addition of such a compelling plot interaction . . .

Without the empowerment of a strong villain to blame for the negative events . . .

Of life . . .

The Bible wouldn't have had the added power of an addictive storyline. A powerful antagonist, such as the malicious Devil, gives the faithful someone to hate, someone to fight against, someone to blame. And, thereupon, this craft technique also serves to sharply define an evil characterization whom the faithful can hold responsible for the world's many woes . . .

And thus it shifts the "finding fault for life's problems" away from the loving omniscient creator . . .

Per adding in an evil victimizer so as to

rationalize the suffering of the world.

In other words, if there is no Devil, then whom would the faithful have to blame for the death of innocent children . . .

For the plagues . . .

Of so many pandemics . . .

For the decay of morals?

The shaman-clerics, of course, have avoided blaming God, have they not? And, consequently, they've had to thus fictionalize someone whom they could blame.

So, per this clarity of theological intent, religious dualism can thus be considered to be nothing more than another fanciful creation of the imagination. For clearly, this is true because God (and only God) could have created the Devil since the Bible states that God created everything in the universe.

But wait.

If God did create such an evil force, then doesn't this also prove that God is not a compassionate and loving deity . . .

Since it means that God is responsible for creating evil, i.e., for creating the Devil?

Or, another way of stating the obvious, what loving father would choose to bring into existence an evil force that had the ability to harm his own children?

Now, when analyzed further, the theologians would also have us believe that this moral contradiction wasn't God's intent, in that they would claim that God created evil (and the Devil) so as to tempt man and thus weed out the bad seed from the good seed.

But . . .

Is this religious doctrine at all logical . . .

For why would God want to create any bad seed at all . . .

If he's truly a loving creator?

So the explanation that God created evil in order to test us is simply a flawed rationalization for dualism. And to be clear, it's also our opinion that this fictional theology is, in actuality, a well-contrived evasion that's been designed to fit the needs of the clergy so as to buttress their imagined dogmas. For when such nonsensical explanations are employed to reinforce the clergy's illogical dogma . . .

When such centerpieces of the clergy's thought philosophies have no scientific or rational foundations . . .

The shaman-clerics have but few rhetorical options that they can employ in order to defend their . . .

Superstitious fantasies . . .

Other than hiding behind the common manufactured dictum of:

"The average person cannot hope to

understand the vastness of God's intent, and thus the public has no choice but to rely upon faith when asking such questions."

Now, of course, such statements of avoidance are amazingly opportune, are they not? What if a Nobel laureate used a similar excuse per his nuclear-bomb research? When asked why a certain atomic particle rapidly achieved an electron decay, what if the scientist said: "I don't know. That's just the way it is. You have to rely on faith and simply believe what I'm telling you is the honest truth."

But . . .

Being the skeptics that we are . . .

We refuse to accept such self-serving religious explanations when it comes to mainstream theology . . .

Because understanding the motivations as to why the Biblical storytellers were compelled to generate an antagonistic villain to oppose God . . .

And thereby pondering why the holy scribes chose to enhance their fictions by generating the theological framework for what came to be known as dualism . . .

Reveals a telling truth that should not be hidden from the faithful.

Therein, having attempted to illuminate one of the more potent theological fabrications, let us now proceed to a corollary Biblical fallacy.

In regards to God's physicality, it's instructive to note . . .

That a majority . . .

Of the faithful believe . . .

That God . . .

Actually resides in heaven, i.e., . . .

Many religions promote the belief that heaven is a wonderful place . . .

Which they've been taught is unreachable by "living" human beings . . .

Whereas the Devil lives in hell, i.e., . . .

Lives in a totally hideous place that sinners will be sent upon their death?

But when one applies an objective analysis to this "postmortem" dogma . . .

Isn't it highly convenient that both of these extreme locations are unverifiable to science?

And isn't this fanciful theology of heaven and hell . . .

Yet another instance of the shaman-clerics employing a dramatic storytelling technique, i.e., . . .

Of designing a philosophical framework that serves to enhance the splendor of their protagonist (God) and, at the same time, to darken the evil persona of his antagonist (the Devil)?

And it should also be noted that, per this theology, wayward souls (i.e., unrepentant nonbelievers) . . .

Will be forced to endure the endless punishment of burning in hell. For haven't the masses been taught that if they don't believe in God's holy message . . .

That the faithful's unseen God (in heaven) will smite such sinners and thus confine them to a monstrous hell?

But yet . . .

If this line of reasoning . . .

Is to be believed . . .

Then this also means that God created the universe . . .

And designed it so that one of his heavenly angels would become the Devil . . .

But yet . . .

Per the Biblical record, God was also responsible for creating man's DNA, was he not? So if this is true . . .

Then wouldn't such a religious reality also mean that God created a string of chromosomes . . .

Which, in fact, causes humans to stray from his holy message via the temptation of sin . . .

But then . . .

When such "sinners" do fall from grace and thus commit immoral acts . . .

The clergy would have us believe that God is also responsible for creating a special punishment for these sinful humans . . .

In that . . .

God has willed into existence a place the clergy calls hell, a place for sinners to be punished, a place for the sinful members of God's creation to suffer the divine consequences of their immoral acts?

But . . .

If viewed objectively, does this "theology of opposites" make any sense at all? For what loving parent . . .

Would want their child to be flawed with the weakness of immoral action?

And clearly, if a parent could design their own child's DNA . . .

What parent would intentionally select a set of "amoral" chromosomes, which would then cause their child to perform sinful deeds?

Also . . .

What type of parent would then proceed to design a hellish punishment to torture their sinfully dysfunctional child . . .

A child that the parent had intentionally created with flawed DNA?

In other words, is there any logic to this hellish intent? Why would an omnipotent creator design such an environment for his human offspring . . .

Or is this yet another fantasy, which has been imagined by status-seeking Biblical creative thinkers . . .

Who have slyly crafted a complex web of theological dogmas by conceptualizing their own ego needs . . .

In that such a hellish fiction is obviously a human creation that's been imagined and manufactured by the overlording clergy in order to proselytize their addictive thought control over the masses?

For isn't it apparent that the concept of people burning in hell . . .

Was designed to be so frightening . . .

So repulsive . . .

That the masses would be awed into conforming to the clergy's will? And, as we've previously established, doesn't the clergy reap a self-serving gain by advocating such a pernicious nightmare?

Of course, per this theology, if a person wants to avoid burning in hell . . .

They can do so by kowtowing to the will of the shaman-clerics . . .

For isn't it the clergy's desire to satisfy their own needs . . .

And not the will of God . . .

That's the true reason why the masses have been indoctrinated with this devilish thought control?

And so . . .

Just as there is no God . . .

There also is no Devil, and there's no hell.

Yet, depending upon one's level of religious indoctrination . . .

We're cognizant of the fact that the vast majority of those who've been taught these addictive dogmas . . .

Will not be able to easily withdraw from their thought dependency. It will even take an extended amount of time for the highly educated to deprogram their cognition . . .

Because . . .

For most people . . .

A pernicious religious conditioning has been embedded deep within . . .

Their psyches . . .

Regardless of their educational level.

IX

The Harmful Benefits of Religious Addiction

Most would agree that mankind, in general, has garnered numerous social benefits from the mainstream religions . . .

In that many shaman-clerics have, throughout the ages, advocated a philosophy of goodwill between all members of society.

And, in this regard, most would also agree that this benevolent attitude has been promoted per an honest desire to help the less fortunate. But yet . . .

It's also true . . .

That when religions employ social caring as a core element of their spiritual dogma . . .

Such an advocacy does not, in and of itself, offer any proof that there is a God.

For truly, there have been numerous non-religious communities, which have been formed throughout history, that have also advocated charitable deeds. Worldwide, there are an abundance of nonaffiliated food banks, charitable organizations, and community action committees . . .

All of which have helped the less fortunate, and many of these have never been associated with a god dogma.

So . . .

Per an analysis of the historical record, we are of the opinion that human beings have a natural desire to . . .

Help the disadvantaged . . .

Offer assistance to the poor . . .

Show concern for the less fortunate . . .

And . . .

We also feel that these concerns of nonpartisan humanism did not evolve from the various religious systems of the world . . .

But did, in fact, predate such philosophies and were then co-opted by the various religious applications that subsequently followed.

Human beings are social animals. The benefits and rewards of protecting and supporting the other members of a tribe . . .

Have a genetic foundation, just as similar activity can be found in the helpful social skills of various animal groups.

Wolves live in supportive packs, as do apes. A willingness to share and assist the less fortunate . . .

Is not a religious concept at all . . .

Because it's a natural survival mechanism, which is inherent in many animals and which is also inherent in our DNA (which is 96% the same as the hairy apes).

And, of course, there are those among us who've lived long enough and who've also developed an insightful view of their fellow humans . . .

To know that some of the most caring, warmhearted, and considerate . . .

Individuals . . .

Do not belong to any church, synagogue, or mosque . . .

And yet . . .

Many such nonreligious individuals make significant donations to numerous charities.

Conversely, it's also our opinion that a significant number of the most fervent individuals who are compelled to vocalize their faith and, in so doing, profess to be strong believers in either the Torah or the Bible or the Koran . . .

Such fundamentalists . . .

Can also be highly hypocritical when it

comes to their own self-serving actions.

And though we agree that religions do motivate their congregations to perform charitable deeds -- there is, at times, a hateful dark side to most of the mainstream thought philosophies. Specifically, religious dogmas have precipitated numerous mass murderers.

Osama bin Laden (a devote Muslim who orchestrated the World Trade Center attack) and Timothy McVeigh (a believing Catholic who bombed the Oklahoma City Federal Building) . . .

Are two such examples.

Of course when such deplorable acts are linked to mainstream dogmas, the theologians will immediately take issue and counter such an accusation . . .

By stating that these evildoers, even though they were faithful believers . . .

Were not at all representative of their religion and thus were acting outside of their doctrines. And the clergy will also make the argument that any religious philosophy can be misinterpreted and misused by deranged people.

Now, of course, we absolutely agree. Most religious laws are not precisely followed by the majority of world's so-called believers. Hence, a large number of believers are simply self-serving hypocrites when it comes to a dedicated adherence to the tenets of their religion.

In a word, even though the mainstream religions advocate a number of well-meaning moral principles, these admonishments are frequently ignored . . .

Which brings us to yet another dogmatic question. For God to be fully responsible for man's creation and yet not responsible for man's evil actions . . .

How can such a dichotomy of intent be true? Did God intentionally create evil . . .

Or did he not?

And remember, if the theologians are to be believed, God cannot be irresponsible, i.e., God must be fully responsible for all of his actions.

Nevertheless, these same theologians are not able, for some reason, to clearly explain why the world is plagued by evil actions, are they?

Hence, if there is a God, then he would have to be completely responsible for all of his creation -- would he not? -- since everything on Earth came into existence per his willful intention.

Now, per this context, the clergy has also attempted to mitigate this gapping theological flaw by promoting the concept of "free will" . . .

In that the clerics would have us believe that God has a desire for us to make independent decisions . . .

When it comes to our fates . . .

For even though God designed the universe and was also the "intelligent designer" of all life on Earth . . .

He should not be blamed for the tragedies of innocent children dying in Third World countries, nor should he be held responsible for the mass murders . . .

Of thousands of people.

The theological concept that states that God designed humans to have a non-subservient will to God's will . . .

And of man being responsible for his own actions . . .

This religious thesis is key to God being considered a compassionate creator while, at the same time, not at all responsible for any of humanity's suffering. So the clergy would have us believe that the evil in the world . . .

Is not God's fault . . .

But rather is the work of the Devil.

Yet, if this doctrine of "free will" is to be believed -- then man is free to choose good over evil, is he not? And isn't this the holy dogma that the mainstream clerics have declared to be absolutely true, in that they've repeatedly stated that God doesn't want to control the incremental actions of man?

And to further clarify, haven't the mainstream theologians also clearly stated that an individual controls his or her own fate per God having granted humankind "free will"?

Of course, by declaring that God has granted everyone "free will," haven't the clerics also proceeded to design a convenient loophole in regards to rationalizing the theology of why some individuals can be tempted by the Devil and why other individuals have the fortitude and "will" to avoid temptation?

Moreover, isn't this holy dogma completely misunderstood by the masses . . .

For if "free will" truly exists . . .

Then why do people pray to God and plead with him to save them from evil? Do not such believers realize that God's intent is to allow "free will"? So if a person does, in fact, have "free will" . . .

Then it is not God who decides an individual's fate . . .

Since it would appear that a person seals his or her own fate via individual action . . .

In that God, having excluded himself from any intercession per his creation of "free will" . . .

Cannot intervene in order to help an individual since God has granted everyone the ability to choose their own fate . . .

Has he not?

So . . .

If God is unwilling to intervene in order to save a sick child or to smite an invading enemy per the concept of "free will" . . .

Regardless of the fact that "believers in God" may pray for his intercession (in such cases) . . .

And regardless of the fact that these same faithful practitioners of religion will suffer due to God's inaction . . .

Because, per the doctrine of "free will" -- their prayers will not prevent the loss of a child to an illness . . .

Or stop a group of invading soldiers from massacring an entire family . . .

Even though the soldiers may be faithful believers in the same God.

Indeed, if the theologians are correct in their interpretation of divine dogma, then God is "free" to allow harmful events to happen to any of his believers, is he not?

So ultimately, isn't this what "free will" actually means?

Doesn't it actually mean that God is "free" to ignore the prayers of his faithful?

Hence, it's our opinion that "free will," when viewed objectively, is actually nothing more than another invented rationalization, which has been employed by the clergy in order to explain away the inconsistencies of invented dogma.

Or, to clarify the obvious:

Can the theologians actually prove that God has intentionally established a system of "free will"?

No. They cannot.

Such a proof isn't doable, for there isn't any validating science that can substantiate the premise that "free will" does actually exist, is there?

"Free will" is simply an imagined fantasy.

Now, of course, if the theologians are asked to clarify why they think that God has granted mankind "free will" -- they may reference the mystery of their faith or invoke their holy book (i.e., either the Bible or the Koran) as proof that their claim is factual.

But does the Bible even offer any verifiable proof as to its own validity, much less the validity of "free will"?

Indeed, to repeat yet again . . .

How do we even know that the stories written in the Bible or in the Koran are true and thus are not imagined fictions?

Is there any solid scientific proof that verifies the referenced miraculous events in either text?

And think about this. If God's intent is for us to fully understand his holy message and thus to follow his intended laws (as advocated by the various clerics of numerous faiths) . . .

Then why didn't God put in place verifiable scientific proofs so as to confirm all of the Biblical events and thus muzzle his skeptics? Surely God had the power to do so, did he not?

Conversely, if we are correct and the Bible is nothing more than superstitious stories . . .

Stories that have been interwoven with a few well-placed historical facts . . .

Then isn't it obvious why certain prayers only "appear" to be fulfilled, however infrequently . . .

Due to the statistical probability of having a proportional number of sudden reversals occur in everyday life?

Moreover -- if the Bible is correct, then why did God's so-called major miracles only occur in the Middle East, and why did these great events only involve a relatively small number of tribes?

What about the millions of people who lived in the other continents of the world outside of the Middle East? And what about God's present-day believers?

Why has God . . .

(Considered by the faithful to be a supreme being via having interceded with so many divine actions in the Biblical stories, stories which took place thousands of years ago) . . .

So . . .

Why has God . . .

Continually avoided any verifiable scientific interaction with mankind in modern times?

Remember, if the Bible is to be believed, God instigated -- in ancient times -- a number of major miracles, did he not?

Specifically, the Bible states that God spoke to his chosen prophets . . .

And that God punished mankind by causing a huge flood . . .

And that God laid to waste the walls of Jericho . . .

To name but a few. The Bible and the Koran also proclaim that there were many other breathtaking events, which also occurred only because God chose to intercede in order to assist his believing faithful.

God parted the Red Sea.

God placed Jesus in Mary's womb.

God lifted Muhammad up into heaven.

So if these holy books are, indeed, true and if these miracles did, in fact, actually occur . . .

Then wouldn't this also mean that God's "free will" is selectively applied . . .

In that, at certain times, he's willing to insert his divine will and thus change the fate of a few of his believers . . .

And yet at other times, God chooses not to get involved at all?

So if the miraculous events in the Bible and the Koran did happen, then why hasn't God continued to perform such impressive miracles in our own day and age?

And clue?

Could the answer be . . .

It's because 21st century man has developed sophisticated scientific instruments, which can easily debunk any false religious claims . . .

Because when such superstitious fictions are invoked today . . .

Our educated press and enlightened governments have the ability to mount insightful investigations that can easily discern what the actual facts are, as opposed to having the myth creators generate what they want us to believe the facts are? In short, have there ever been any scientifically proven religious miracles (certified by academia) to bolster God's existence?

Or, to restate the obvious, wouldn't most rational individuals assume . . .

That the clergy should have been able to "scientifically document" at least one miraculous event via a video camera . . .

By this point in history?

Furthermore, isn't it also true that anyone can claim that God spoke to him (or her) . . .

Or claim that praying to God caused a miracle to happen . . .

Since such pronouncements are relatively easy to make, are they not?

Of course they are . . .

In that anyone can claim that God "did this" or that God "did that."

Yet such unverified assertions do not actually prove that a miraculous event did occur, do they?

Hence, as with any human interaction, self-serving falsehoods have to always be considered as primary possibilities in regards to a holy declaration . . .

Or to a claim that a godly miracle has taken place. For, unquestionably, in today's world of scientific-based logic . . .

We should be highly suspicious of any

religious claims that can't be legitimately verified. Of course many well-educated people are quite cognizant of the fact that all of the so-called miraculous events that were depicted in the Bible and in the Koran . . .

Were, in fact, nothing more than the imagined fantasies of superstitious minds. Our modern scholars are also cognizant of the fact that, at the time that the Bible and the Koran were written, there were no impartial investigatory systems in existence, i.e., . . .

No one applied scientific analysis in order to vet the supernatural claims that the ancient religious scribes professed. When the Bible's mysterious events were first verbalized vis-à-vis campfire stories long before they were actually . . .

Written down . . .

There were no fact checkers to certify the truthfulness of such claims, nor were there any federal investigators to confirm the honesty of the claimants. And neither did any advanced forensic technology exist (e.g., there were no lie detectors, no truth serums, and no voice analyzers).

Yet now, in our present age of logic (and of verifiable science) -- a majority of the faithful is still reluctant to question the truthfulness of the Holy Bible.

Strange, is it not?

X

What God Forgot to Tell His Holy Prophets

Human beings are, for the most part, caring and considerate . . .

Per their instinctual inclination to socialize, in that the average person has a natural predisposition towards "moral" interaction. Of course the desire to conform to a fair-and-impartial governing system is easily understandable . . .

Because such social technologies function to counteract life's random negativities and serve to protect an individual from unfair aggressions . . .

Either from inside a tribe . . .

Or from an opposing community. For clearly -- we, as individuals, derive innumerable benefits from being members of a unified group.

Moreover, it's also our opinion that the human race has an innate inclination to engage in ethical actions . . .

Which means that the clergy doesn't have a moral prerogative to enforce religious dogma that modifies a person's negative desires. In our modern age, civil networks have assumed this moral function . . .

With our advanced social rules and governmental laws being able to effectively govern our aggressions via mitigating our self-serving desires . . .

And thus these civil enforcements are fundamental to any well-functioning society. Conversely, when people are allowed to wantonly pursue their animalistic urges, such unrestrained expressions weaken the societal glue and can cause reverberating conflict.

Now . . .

It's also true that mankind's humanness is somewhat ambiguous when it comes to the interaction of charitable deeds . . .

Since individuals do not always choose to do what's best for others . . .

Because many people are unable to ignore their inner urges. Indeed, deep inside all of us, there's the constant tug of the "me" appetite, which can nag us into breaking the rules via a desire to instantly gratify our selfish will. But . . .

Equally . . .

There's also the empowerment of our embedded social programming . . .

That's been derived from our families and communities . . .

And thus this social conditioning can negate our self-serving egos and modify our will . . .

Motivating us to deny our immediate urges in order to reap the interpersonal gains of conformity. Also, as is common knowledge, Eastern religions tend to be more accepting of our primitive dark sides. The orient's concept of yin/yang actually factors in an added tolerance for our selfish imperfections.

For example, in the Buddhist faith, it's understood that we all have positive and negative impulses. And so . . .

When one strives to become a good Buddhist, one doesn't have to deny one's inner weaknesses, but rather one is introduced to instructional applications, which can be engaged to control and modify the willful negative urges.

Plus . . .

It should also be noted that Western religions tend to characterize the natural self as a negative . . .

And thus controlling dogmas have been designed, which function to repress our willful urges.

Here's an example. In the Christian faith, when someone disobeys one of God's rules, this person is considered a sinner. And, in a broader sense, all of mankind, per Christian dogma . . .

Is said to have fallen from grace because our earliest ancestors (Adam and Eve) supposedly strayed from God's will . . .

And so now all of their offspring (which includes the whole human race) should acknowledge mankind's communal sin and ask for forgiveness. This is the Western concept of "original sin."

It should also be noted that "original sin" was specifically designed by the clergy to transfer a nagging guilt into the faithfuls' collective consciousness. And, therein, it's per this "guilt" dogma that a number of our primal urges have been declared to be defective . . .

In that most congregations have been taught that true believers have no choice but to continually strive to jettison their animal passions in order for them to be able to conform to God's divine wishes.

Moreover, if the theologians are correct

in this regard, then God has, in effect, designed a theology, which intentionally places the clergy in control of a person's willful thoughts per the employment of a negative-reinforcing dogma . . .

Which functions as a mitigator to an individual's animal instincts.

Hence, we have an interesting paradox, do we not? For if mainstream dogma truly reflects God's intent, then why did God "create" individuals with "flawed" desires in the first place, i.e., why does our DNA cause us to have such sinful obsessions?

Why indeed?

Of course . . .

Most would agree that societies do, in fact, function best when self-serving urges are controlled and modified.

And true, certain religious do's and don'ts are, in many cases, effective tools in infusing a level of moral control into the masses . . .

But such rules of behavior (i.e., moralities) are not inherently religious at all. When properly taught in the formative years of childhood, civilized societies can achieve a more consistent adherence to social laws and can also better protect the public welfare from wayward individuals when "positive" reinforcement is used via the scientific method of honestly explaining why so many people have such urges (as opposed to reverting to the superstitious guilt of "original sin").

Also, it's instructive to note that the clergy has, via usurping such judgmental power, proceeded to falsely assume the role of "overlording adjudicators of our will." And, per such action, they have (by enforcing their superstitious indoctrinations) . . .

Become a self-appointed social jury to all sinners (which includes everyone since, per Christian doctrine, we have all sinned) . . .

And thus it's vis-à-vis this dogmatic configuration that the clergy has been able to create the illusion that they are God's earthly administrators, i.e., . . .

The shaman-clerics have assumed the role of holy go-betweens, in that they've been able to deceive the masses into paying them a financial compensation (which supposedly allows the faithful to stay in God's good graces).

In other words . . .

If humans were born with a natural propensity to conform to God's intent . . .

Then what function would the clergy have to serve . . .

For without our tendency to sin, how would the clergy sustain their status and income?

And remember, being a member of the clergy is a career choice . . .

As is being employed as a lawyer, doctor, or carpenter. And, as such . . .

The clergy must have a means of garnering an income . . .

In that they, too, are motivated by a desire to put food on their table . . .

For, as we all know, in modern times God doesn't sprinkle manna from heaven in order to fill the stomachs of the clergy. Instead, it's the members of a clergy's congregation who pay the bills and salaries of a church, synagogue, or mosque. Which brings up yet another interesting historical point in regards to how income was derived by the priests of early Judaism.

Few may know what actually transpired at the original Hebrew Temple in ancient Israel in regards to priestly income . . .

For even back then food was not free.

When the Hebrew faithful were told to bring sacrifices to the Temple in order to prove their allegiance to God's will . . .

Sacrifices such as goats, sheep, birds, and young calves . . .

These were the blood sacrifices that the priests demanded be brought to the Temple. And the Jewish faithful were also taught that the only place that they could worship God was at the Hebrew Temple . . .

For at that time there were no synagogues (and the faithful did not, in fact, pray outside of the Temple).

So it was the Hebrew priests who dictated how the faithful could communicate with God. And having such control over their congregation, the priests declared, in order for a believer to stay in God's good graces . . .

That such a person must bring an animal to the Temple for holy slaughter.

But why?

Why would God need a faithful believer to kill an innocent animal in order to prove his allegiance to God's will? What logic would there be for God to rely on such a proof? In other words, wouldn't God, via his omniscient understanding, already know the actions and thoughts of all of his believers?

But, of course, there was an important reason why the Hebrew priests demanded that the faithful bring sacrifices to the Temple, and it involved what happened to the edible meat after the sacrificial rituals were performed.

That's right. Such sacrificial meats . . .

Were, in fact, eaten by the Temple priests . . .

And were not consumed by God (even though some of the faithful may have thought otherwise).

Also . . .

It should be pointed out that if such sacrifices were not forthcoming . . .

Then how would the Temple priests have been able to fill their bellies . . .

For these men of God didn't work in a merchant trade that generated a barter income, which they could use to garner food, did they?

No, the trade that the Temple priests were employed in was the one of enforcing their mind control over God's believers. Or, another way of stating the obvious:

The Hebrew priests plied the theological trade of religious propaganda. They didn't have to labor in the fields in order to put food on their table; they only had to labor in the minds of the faithful in order to fill their bellies.

Which brings up yet another interesting question. How does the present-day clergy derive their income? Aren't their bills also paid via the same method, in that the blood sacrifice has now evolved from that of a food source into one of a cash donation?

So aren't these modern shamans still laboring in the minds of the faithful in order to put food on their tables?

Mystifying, is it not?

But true.

Moreover, this enforcement of the "faith tax" brings up yet another intriguing question. Today, what would happen if the majority of people were morally pure and had the ability to directly communicate with God?

Or, to reword the question, how would our modern clergy generate an income if there was no sin, i.e., what would happen if God's holy rules were easily adhered to by all of the faithful? How would the clergy pay their bills?

Any idea?

Indeed, this truly is an intriguing question, is it not? Of course if members of the clergy were asked this question, we surmise that they wouldn't be able to offer a logical response . . .

For ironically, the clergy has a vested interest in keeping the masses dependent on sin . . .

For without sin, the clergy wouldn't have an income, would they? Which generates yet another intriguing inconsistency in regards to God's holy intent.

Does it truly seem logical (or even probable) that an all-powerful God would want his faithful to go to war over opposing dogmas . . .

For surely God would not have chosen to enlighten the clergy in one country with a precise and exact holy message . . .

But then later, for some unfathomable reason, God was compelled to change his mind and offer a completely different version of his holy intent to yet another group of believers in a faraway land?

In other words, why would God intentionally communicate a series of inconsistent dogmas? Is there any logic whatsoever to such a scenario?

But remember, if the Christian Bible is to be believed, Jesus Christ was a Hebrew, i.e., a believing Jew who lived in Israel during the time that the Romans controlled the Holy Land. And during this colonial age, even though the Roman Empire was pagan, the Romans of that epoch did, in fact, allow the peoples of the countries that they had invaded . . .

To continue to adhere to whatever religious system the indigenous populace had previously believed in . . .

As long as such religious practices didn't interfere with the Roman administration.

So, as is commonly known, Israel was the birthplace of Christ and also the birthplace of the Christian thought system, in that Christ was not born of Mary in Rome.

Now, at a later date -- when the First Crusade was initiated (a little over a thousand years after Christ's death) -- Hebrew Israel had by then been overrun by Muhammad's Islam . . .

And thus the Diaspora had dispersed most of the Jews to other lands . . .

Which meant that there were, at that time, only a few communities of Christians and Jews left in the Holy Land during the First Crusade. Moreover, it was per this reversal of ideological fortune that a historic irony was precipitated . . .

Because the Europeans felt religiously motivated to send their Christian knights to invade the Holy Land with the intent of establishing the rule of Christ in the country of his birth.

So . . .

Per this unfolding of events, Christ's religion had failed in its own homeland (i.e., in its very birthplace) . . .

And now the Christian faithful (from a faraway land) felt that there was a need to right the wrong.

However, when one considers the Muslim point of view, in that (at that time in history) the Islamic clergy fully believed that their system of thought was the only true version of God's intent and that the Christian invaders were infidels . . .

A theological conundrum proceeded to occur, which highlights the obvious illogic of the possibility that all three of the mainstream religions could be dogmatically correct . . .

Because the priests in the Hebrew Temple (long before) had never accepted the schism which had been advocated by Jesus Christ . . .

Yet several hundred years later, when the Holy See in Rome had decided to establish its own version of Christ's message, asserting that the Roman Catholic Church's concept of God's intent (vis-à-vis their "European" understanding of the holy gospel) was absolutely infallible . . .

Which was in direct opposition to the Judaic belief in a future messiah . . .

And which was also contrary to the teachings of Islam. For when the crusades took place, the Muslim imams were aggressively proselytizing the Christians and Jews, attempting to convert them to Muhammad's true message as revealed to him by Allah.

Now, consequently, per this confluence

of opposing dogmas, the true faithful (i.e., those who'd willing professed a belief in God) . . .

Had a choice of three inconsistent religious doctrines. But, of course, all three of these mainstream dogmas could not, in fact, be the true intent of God. Someone had to have gotten it wrong. And surely it wasn't God . . .

For why would God have intentionally created such a theological inconsistency?

Yet -- for a very long time each of these three great religions have, in fact, advocated that their particular brand of God's revealed message was absolutely true.

But . . .

If there's only one God . . .

Then how is it possible for God to have offered three inconsistent dogmas? Wouldn't such confusion have contradicted his primary intent (assuming that this was his intent) . . .

Of wanting his religious message to be clearly understood by all peoples of the world?

Moreover, who believes that a loving God would cause millions of his faithful to die fighting over incompatible religions . . .

Religions that the shaman-clerics have claimed were transferred directly to their prophets by . . .

God?

But this is, indeed, what actually did occur and continues to occur, is it not?

Yet -- where's the logic in such intent? Why would God have created three opposing dogmas?

Now, admittedly, few people are even willing to ponder such inconsistencies of faith. But when a person does seek such answers . . .

They will, inevitably, be told that the clergy is infallible.

Of course, the bigger irony is that all of the mainstream religions are nothing more than evolved superstitions. For even though these mythic philosophies employ an addictive methodology of certainty . . .

Per their compulsion to convert the masses to their unique belief system . . .

(While proclaiming that all other religions are wrong . . .)

Such assertions of their "will to power" serve to clarify the hidden intent of all three philosophies . . .

In that all three of the mainstream religions are, in actuality, simply conveying a desire to control people's thoughts and thus assert the clergy's power over the masses . . .

And, consequently, this dogmatic overlording is, in truth . . .

Nothing more than a form of mass ego assertion by the shaman-clergy . . .

In that they are nothing more than a falsely informed group of theologians who've embedded their religious teachings with their own alpha domination . . .

By employing an authoritarian willfulness, which has been carefully crafted into a widespread social expression via the use of addictive superstitions. So sadly, the masses have been unknowingly brainwashed into believing such fanciful fictions. And though reasoned proofs can be offered to the contrary, such religious indoctrinations are extremely hard to deprogram via scientific logic. And it should also be noted that at various times in history, a variety of religious mind controls have, in fact, become so pervasive that a number of cult leaders have actually been able to persuade whole congregations to commit mass suicide.

This happened with the Israelites when they were surrounded by the Romans at Masada during the Jewish-Roman War in the first century. Instead of surrendering their ego turf to the European pagans, the Hebrews at Masada chose death.

And a similar event happened with the

Branch Dravidians at Waco in 1993 . . .

And with the naïve faithful at Jonestown in Guyana in 1978.

Yet such religious brainwashing isn't only limited to fringe cults. If the truth be known -- all of the mainstream religions are nothing more than mature cults (having, through repetitive practice, been formalized, ritualized, and accepted into civilized societies) . . .

And thus . . .

The public has been slow to comprehend how totally fixating such indoctrinations into magical thinking can be.

Of course, the public's abhorrence and rejection of overly bizarre religious practices does solidify, somewhat . . .

When law enforcement agencies respond to public concerns . . .

Or when the media applies the "cult label" to the more nontraditional systems of thought (or to the disavowed schismatic offshoots of a mainstream religion).

Castigating nouveau dogmas tends to be much more socially acceptable . . .

Than having our courts question the authenticity of our well-established religions.

And admittedly, as we've previously stated, even the highly educated can be seduced by conformity and swayed by peer pressure . . .

Via the compulsion to find fault with others so as to avoid being ostracized themselves . . .

In that few want to face the mob mentality that can occur when the unconventional actions of nonconformists become known by the public . . .

In that . . .

It's much easier to point a finger at . . .

Cult nonconformity . . .

And thus be seduced into ignoring the historical fact that all religions, at their inception, began as small cults, i.e., began as nonconforming radical thought systems.

Indeed, we find this truth to be highly ironic because, if the Biblical scholars are correct . . .

Then Christ's own ministry had also begun as a small nonconforming cult . . .

For didn't Jesus commence preaching his version of God's message with only twelve disciples by his side? And weren't Christ's beliefs, at that time, considered to be totally unorthodox . . .

In that Jesus was rebelling against the more traditional Hebrew dogma . . .

In that Jesus Christ was very much a nonconforming radical . . .

Since, per the Biblical text . . .

Didn't most of the Hebrew conformists whom Jesus attempted to sway . . .

Shun his message?

And it should also be pointed out, in regards to some of the early Jewish prophets who preached their own holy gospels long before Christ was born . . .

And who were, in fact, the original founders of the Judeo cult . . .

That they, too, were considered to be anti-establishment radicals when they first began their proselytizing. For when Judaism was initially being formulated, mainstream thinking was completely dominated by the preceding pagan beliefs. So, by historical standards, change is an unrelenting constant when it comes to religion. The world has been regularly propagandized by a continual evolution of religious dogma throughout the ages. And such schisms . . .

Have repeatedly occurred in the Judeo-Christian belief system . . .

With one of the more well-known off-shoots being Martin Luther's Protestantism. Luther's Reformation against certain religious teachings (which he himself had been indoctrinated with) . . .

Was truly an attempt to "reform" the

Catholic doctrine. But preceding this rebellion, i.e., in the 900 years before the Reformation . . .

Most defiant Catholics feared the wrath of excommunication and feared being burned at the stake as heretics . . .

And thus censored their skepticisms in order not to be killed or shunned.

Of course . . .

Religious dogma had continually evolved even before the Reformation . . .

For it was roughly 600 years . . .

After Christ . . .

That Muhammad advocated his revolutionary schism . . .

Which was, in fact, simply an ideological derivation that initially had had limited appeal because Muhammad's revelations were not instantly accepted by those in power in the Arab lands. In a word, when Muhammad first proclaimed that he was a prophet of God, few believed him.

So religious scholars are well aware of the fact that the world's most addictive thought systems were not transferred by God to mankind vis-à-vis fully formed dogmas. When the historical record is reviewed, a reoccurring circumstance presents itself . . .

In that all of the mainstream religions

were, in fact, initiated by nonconforming individuals who faced the overwhelming task of proselytizing their holy messages to unbelieving skeptics. And so, per this context, the reality that God's "holy" transmissions have constantly changed via evolving circumstances . . .

Should serve as a red flag as to why such religious ideologies were first originated . . .

For if these so-called God messages were truly sent down from heaven -- then why, at various moments in the past, did God only select a handful of people to function as his holy messengers in order to transfer his divine intent to the masses? In other words, if we are to believe the propagators of the mainstream religions, God -- for some unknown reason -- limited his direct contact to but a chosen few . . .

And only communicated with these select prophets . . .

Employing them as divine advocates to preach his godly intent to others.

Mystifying, is it not? For why, if God's intent was to truly bring all of humanity into his fold . . .

Then why would God have only used such an indirect . . .

And slow means of transmission . . .

As that of communicating with only a handful of prophets . . .

For if there truly is an all-knowing and all-powerful God . . .

And if he has a desire to enlighten the human race with his holy intent . . .

Then why would he not have sent a precise and clearly understood message to thousands of prophets at the exact same moment in time?

Or, if God really wanted to quickly offer his spiritual knowledge to the whole world -- why wouldn't he simply have employed telepathy and thus have communicated directly with all human beings in one miraculous instance?

Wouldn't such a mass transference have made much more sense than the sporadic and inconsistent revelations, which have been dispersed throughout the ages by the shaman-prophets?

Conversely, if certain deluded individuals, throughout history, have had the verbal dexterity to convince those around them that their mental illness was not an affliction . . .

But rather was a holy message from an unseen God . . .

Is this not a much more probable scenario?

Of course . . .

Such logic would be adamantly disputed by the theologians and would be considered blasphemous by the clergy. And surely the shaman-clerics would, without a doubt, label this type of thinking as heresy because such a candid truth clearly erodes their thought myth, negates their power, and pulls income out of their pockets, does it not? Plus, the cleric-theologians might also proceed to dispute such an assertion . . .

By referencing their highly constructed religious rationalizations . . .

Of which . . .

None can be supported by science or verifiable history.

Totally perplexing, is it not?

And think about this. The Christian theologians who want us to believe that God created the Earth in order to use it as a testing ground for his chosen people (i.e., as a way to weed the chaff from the grain, so to speak) . . .

Would also have us believe that God placed all of mankind here on this planet . . .

Per a voyeuristic intent of sorts . . .

In that . . .

God wanted to watch the human race maneuver through a maze of temptation . . .

A complex maze that God, himself, had

designed so as to exclude certain types of individuals whom he did not want in heaven.

But why would an omniscient god need to do such a thing? Wouldn't God already have known the particulars . . .

As to whom would eventually live a qualifying life of good deeds . . .

As compared to those who would obviously fail his test and thus not be able to live up to his heavenly standards per not heeding his holy admonitions?

Wouldn't God have known, even before he created the world . . .

Even before he brought his human creatures into existence . . .

Wouldn't such a supreme being have already known the eventual outcome . . .

As to which humans would pass his test and thus be accepted into heaven . . .

As opposed to those who'd be cast down into hell?

For surely there never was a need for any sort of earthly testing at all, was there? God would've already been cognizant as to those who would, in fact . . .

Be tempted by sin . . .

Even before such complexities were added into the earthly equation, would he have not?

In other words, haven't you ever wondered...

Why God created so many...

Sinful people...

For if God had always intended to only offer his reward of heaven...

To only a select few...

Then why did he create so many billions of sinners with flawed DNA? Why has God been testing such a vast number of people if they have little chance whatsoever of ever passing his test? Is that what a loving God would do, or is this weeding-out holy dogma nothing more than a creative fiction which has been generated by the human imagination?

And it should also be noted that the clergy's representation of God's intent appears to have continually evolved via a paralleling progression in man's scientific knowledge. For as the clergy has slowly come to accept the undeniable truths of science...

They've also had to repeatedly reconfigure their dogma in order to have it align with the scientific facts.

But why?

In other words...

If there truly is a God...

Then surely his wisdom would be

infinite and separate from man's evolution, i.e., there's no logical reason to believe that God's knowledge would be dependent upon the clergy's incremental acquisition of scientific understanding, is there?

Yet, the clergy's expression of God's intent has continued to expand vis-à-vis the religious assimilation of scientific truth . . .

Vis-à-vis a similar nonreligious evolution in scientific understanding.

But why has this occurred?

Why didn't God, upon first speaking with Noah (the genetic predecessor to Abraham, a.k.a., the founding father of the three great religions of the world) . . .

Why didn't God enlighten Noah with hard scientific facts, i.e., why didn't God offer Noah some truly advanced scientific knowledge on Mount Ararat?

Or why didn't God tell Abraham that the Earth revolved around the Sun . . .

Or that there were billions of stars in the universe . . .

Or why didn't God explain to his chosen prophets how to prevent the spread of plagues or how to avoid infectious germs?

But this knowledge transference didn't occur, did it?

Why not?

Could it have been because the Biblical

storytellers at that time didn't have such knowledge, and so they were limited (i.e., constrained by their imaginations) as to what they were able to imagine God would truly have said to Noah or Moses or Jesus or Muhammad?

In other words, if the world's great holy books are to be believed, God's scientific knowledge has always appeared to be exceedingly limited, has it not?

And doesn't it seem highly suspicious that God, in the Bible, never transferred to his chosen people any advanced scientific expertise at all?

Thought provoking?

Moreover, why have the theologians avoided this topic, i.e., why haven't they attempted to explain this obvious flaw in God's holy message . . .

For hasn't God, through the ages, only been characterized as offering humanity . . .

A limited (and contemporary) knowledge that's already been commonly known . . .

Without any reference to the advanced discoveries of the distant future?

Specifically -- why did God only transfer fanciful prophecies (i.e., future predictions, which were filled with symbolic wonder and which could easily have been imaged by the Biblical storytellers) . . .

And thus . . .

God did not, as logic would've prescribed, transfer any hard science to his faithful?

Indeed, why has God never offered his believers any advanced scientific knowledge at all, e.g., why has God never transferred to his faithful any insightful instructions on the inner mechanics of the atom or how to increase the crop yields of barren fields?

Is there any logic to God's absolute silence in regards to hard science? But this is what has occurred, is it not?

So, for some unknowable reason, it seems as though God did not enlighten his prophets with any helpful scientific insight. In fact, there's no reference to any advanced scientific knowledge in either the Bible or the Koran, is there?

Of questionable concern?

And yet . . .

Per such obvious limitations of the Bible and the Koran . . .

In regards to advanced knowledge . . .

The evidence of where religious thinking truly originated . . .

Points . . .

Not to God . . .

But to the limited imaginations of the superstitious shamans who generated their false religious dogmas . . .

For when we read such chapters as "The Book of Revelations" in the Christian Bible, it's interesting to note how fanciful the style actually is. Yes, this adjective-rich narrative soars with dream-like flourishes of three-headed beasts, apocalyptical plagues, and worldwide disasters. But there's no mention at all of the scientific discoveries to come, is there?

A true revelation of future events?

No, not at all.

For clearly, it seems as though God only wanted to transfer certain highly stylized what-ifs to mankind and not offer his faithful any hard scientific facts at all.

Yet . . .

In this regard . . .

What would've been of greater value to God's believers? Was it more important to forecast the three-headed beasts to come (which we're still waiting for) . . .

Or would've God's faithful been much better served by having been offered a clear explanation as to the science needed to manufacture penicillin?

Holy prophecy, indeed.

And so . . .

In all honesty . . .

Haven't our minds evolved to the point

where . . .

At least some of us . . .

Are able to read between the lines when evaluating these Biblical fantasies . . .

For surely the intellectuals among us, if allowed to objectively analyze such holy transferences, can plainly see that the Bible's wordsmithing was designed to incite fear in our superstitious ancestors . . .

Because . . .

It's quite obvious that many parts of the Bible were designed with the intent to awe the uneducated masses with God's divine power?

And, in this context, isn't the Biblical derivation from paganism unmistakably evident . . .

For didn't the primitive shamans also use such imaginative narratives to promote fear in their listeners by referencing the amazing feats of deadly beasts such as fire-breathing dragons? And aren't fairy tales rife with similar creations? But what well-educated individual today . . .

Thinks that a fire-breathing dragon ever existed . . .

Other than in the imagination of a creative storyteller?

Or should we believe whatever the shaman-clerics want us to believe, knowing

full well that their agenda is self-serving?
Now . . .
To be impartial and objective . . .
There are certain historical qualifications, which should be referenced . . .
For it does appear as though that a number of the events alluded to in the New Testament -- did, in fact, occur.
But it should also be noted that the most reliable historical chronicle of facts supports the unvarnished truth that the circumstances surrounding Christ's death were simply the normal intrigues of political power (i.e., Roman vs. Hebrew) . . .
And that these events were not caused by any God-induced phenomena of miracles, in that no occurrence of supernatural phenomena actually transpired in regards to the death of a rebel known as Jesus Christ.
For, as we've previously stated, when storytellers are tasked with framing their work within a so-called "oral history" . . .
There's a natural tendency for such fabricators to reference actual tribal members and then to elevate these leaders into heroic protagonists . . .
In that . . .
When storytellers are able to empower their so-called historical events with the heightened craft of literary devices, it serves

to enhance the emotional bond to the narrative. So, through the ages, attention-seeking storytellers have learned that they can up the stakes of their plots by embellishing true events, i.e., by adding in imagined fictions so as to garner a heightened interest in their work . . .

Because such literary mechanisms truly attract a much larger audience . . .

To such texts . . .

Than the uneventful truths of normal life.

XI

Acclimating to Hidden Knowledge Via Religious Withdrawal

We are well aware . . .
    That the hidden knowledge presented via this text . . .
    May be considered . . .
    By some . . .
    To be contentious . . .
    Because religious deconstructionism can be highly thought provoking.
    It's also true that the instructional process offered within these pages may be somewhat troubling for those who, in their childhoods, were indoctrinated with magical thinking. Moreover, when such a book advocates atheism . . .
    And when a reader agrees with the metaphysical arguments presented . . .

If this person has previously been a faithful believer . . .

Then they may, upon assimilating this hidden knowledge, have some difficulty in acquiring the deprogramming tools needed in order to fully counteract the many years of addictive brainwashing. So, in consideration of this possibility, if such a person does progress forward . . .

Via challenging their old beliefs . . .

They may find their evolution into religious deconstructionism . . .

To be almost overwhelming at times. And, if this occurs, then it may be due to the fact that certain religious imprints have been embedded exceptionally deep within their thoughts.

At the same time, others could have a completely different response . . .

In that reactions may vary in regards to our frank analysis of superstitious addiction.

Of course, for some . . .

Our enlightened offering might actually evoke a disorientating uncertainty. And since such a reaction may be strong at first, those who have this occur . . .

And who struggle to understand the hidden knowledge presented herein . . .

Shouldn't be overly concerned . . .

For having such an emotional response is normal when one begins to initiate a truly enlightened perspective . . .

Which challenges so many years of intensive programming. Thereupon, we're quite cognizant of the courage that's needed in order to rebel against one's embedded thoughts . . .

Because the ideological systems that have been implanted within the minds of so many people . . .

Are not easily overcome . . .

In that such addictive thought dependencies can affect a person's judgmental patterns . . .

Per one's comprehension of truth . . .

And per the relevancy of interpersonal structures . . .

Via a person's social status being dependent upon his or her conformity to mainstream dogma. And so . . .

It takes a determined effort in order for an individual to be able to circumvent the numerous thought obstacles that can occur when one seeks enlightened knowledge.

Plus, a heightened concern arises when someone who is deeply religious reads this text and, for the first time, begins to contemplate the overwhelming reality that the holy dogma that they've been taught since early childhood is completely false.

Also, it's assumed that a certain percentage of believers will react with a protective anger as a way of coping with their theological uncertainty, as a way of shielding their dependent egos . . .

In that . . .

We accept the possibility that such people may then transition into a defensive mode via a knee-jerk desire to debate the legitimacies of their magical thinking. For clearly, when strongly held beliefs are challenged, the faithful who possess such beliefs will naturally feel compelled to defend their religious indoctrination. Yet, in all probability . . .

When they do attempt to debate this hidden knowledge . . .

They will have no choice but to employ their own religious programming . . .

And thus . . .

Call upon the same dogmatic addiction that's been embedded in their minds . . .

To engage their argument.

Consequently, just as occurs with members of fringe cults . . .

Such religious defenders may not even be aware of the pervasive thought control that continues to hobble their minds and negate their objectivity . . .

For it's exceptionally hard for such skeptics of thought indoctrination to even be aware of the ingrained mental structures that have been implanted deep within their minds. Of course . . .

Many such individuals are relatively happy with their lives of dogmatic conformity. And this can be especially true for those who've attained an economic abundance that extends well beyond the basic necessities and into an upscale lifestyle. In these cases, overcoming the separation anxiety from magical thinking can be extremely problematic.

However, for the many nonconformists who've had nagging doubts as to the legitimacy of certain religious doctrines . . .

But who've been reluctant to express such thoughts . . .

Per wanting to avoid . . .

Being ostracized . . .

Per wanting to avoid being categorized as an atheist by their family, friends, and neighbors . . .

Such questioning personalities may now realize that they don't have to keep their nonconforming considerations . . .

To themselves . . .

And thus they will, in all probability, welcome the understanding that's being presented via this text.

So -- we're cognizant of the internal/external oppositions that people may face in regards to religious deconstructionism . . .

For such fears are entirely legitimate (even in this day and age of widespread tolerance). And yes, we're also well aware of the prolonged period of time that will be needed to fully comprehend the hidden knowledge presented here . . .

For even the well educated may not, upon first introduction . . .

Be able to completely incorporate such enlightened truth . . .

In that a certain amount of extended contemplation may be required. And in this regard, we also believe that certain delays in the acceptance of this hidden knowledge will be partly due to the inherent problem of challenging addictive thinking at its emotional core . . .

Because the systemic programming that's been embedded in most people's minds (since early childhood) . . .

Involves a number of withdrawal levels.

Plus, it will be doubly hard for those who do not have access to an enlightened support system, i.e., . . .

For certain individuals to mitigate the hardship of attempting such an overwhelming thought transition.

And even though many readers of this text may consider themselves to be open minded and tolerant of new ideas . . .

The practicality of withdrawing from such a pervasive thought addiction can be, at times, de-energizing and emotionally debilitating . . .

For when an individual attempts to extract a deeply embedded cognitive structure that's had the ability to influence their thoughts since childhood . . .

Such addictive dogma can be exceedingly difficult to extricate.

In other words, individuals tend to define their social personas (i.e., their roles in society) . . .

Vis-à-vis a complex web . . .

Of interactions . . .

Which have slowly matured, year-by-year, within their subconscious minds . . .

Beginning at birth . . .

Per responding to the caring concerns of parents (and thus mimicking their elders' thought patterns) . . .

And continuing forward by way of the childhood training that comes when one is taught the cultural values of their social communities . . .

And then finally . . .

Evolving into a person's adult conformity, which allows one to garner the interpersonal coping skills that are needed for long-term survival.

So . . .

There is a considerable amount of social programming to overcome, and it's not at all easy by any means. In fact, it can literally take a number of years to progress through the various levels of enlightened understanding . . .

As small increments of awareness begin to replace . . .

The superstitious imperfections . . .

Because most such seekers of truth will at first be reluctant to completely jettison their belief in God or to challenge the programmed acceptance of their religious dogma. Indeed, few will have the ability to rapidly evolve their thinking by promptly rejecting their socially installed belief system.

Why?

Because such seekers of objective truth are rarely rewarded with positive reinforcements . . .

Since there are but a small number of advocates (and interpersonal support systems) to assist an individual with the deconstruction of religious programming.

Furthermore, a person has to contend with the negative consequences of nonconformity and with the financial disincentives that can occur when one is excluded from the safety net of society's conforming community.

Yet, of course, there are two positive benefits.

There's the heartfelt reward of truth . . .

And there's also the joyous reward of freeing oneself . . .

From the false superstitions . . .

Which have caused so much harm to so many people throughout the ages.

Aubrey M. Horton

Aubrey M. Horton (MFA, UCLA) has consulted on projects for Warner Brothers, Paramount, and HBO. *Creative Screenwriting* magazine rated him as a "highly recommended" script doctor. For the Directors Guild of America, Horton edited five books on Hollywood's Golden Age. In 1987, the Colorado Council on the Arts and Humanities awarded him a prestigious screenwriting fellowship.

To purchase this book on the Web, go to ->

www.createspace.com/3387597

Made in the USA